"Liz Fiedorow Sjaastad bares her soul in this beautifully written book, recounting the trauma of being raised by a mother with untreated schizophrenia and an alcoholic father. Even as a helpless nine-year-old, she knows that taboos around schizophrenia eclipse alcoholism, and she fears becoming her mother who converses with the refrigerator. While her father surrenders to alcoholism after his greatest love morphs into his greatest misery, Sjaastad and her siblings experience their own demons. As successful adults, Sjaastad and her sister again feel helpless as they seek assistance for ailing parents from a health care system that refuses to acknowledge anosognosia, a lack of understanding of one's illness. How they cope is a lesson for us all. I strongly recommend this book."

—**Mindy Greiling,** former state legislator and author of *Fix What You Can: Schizophrenia and a Lawmaker's Fight for Her Son*

"With clear, unapologetic prose, Liz Fiedorow Sjaastad lays bare her family's traumas not in an attempt to garner sympathy or naval gaze but to ask her readers to be witness to what it means to struggle both with others and within oneself. *You're Too Young to Understand* refocuses the telling of an all-too-familiar story of how schizophrenia and generational trauma impacts a family to encompass not only the inherent pain but also the surprising moments of joy. Sjaastad's love for her family members—no matter how frustrating those relationships were—shines, as does her writing."

—**Anika Fajardo,** author of *Magical Realism for Non-Believers: A Memoir of Finding Family*

"*You're Too Young to Understand* opens at the end of a father's life, in a quiet hospital room. In the corner of that room, the author's mother, who lives with schizophrenia, wonders aloud if an injection of Vitamin C might not cure her husband.

This is a book of tiptoes on eggshells. Yet, it is a book of deep beauty: the relationship between Liz Fiedorow Sjaastad and her sister—and the delicate look back into the past—reveal moments of love and a few clues into the mysteries of her parents.

Sjaastad leads the reader through the dying and death of one parent while holding the hand of the other, the one with the mental illness left with all the decision-making control. *You're Too Young to Understand* is a rewarding read for anyone who had a complex childhood relationship with their aging parents, especially as they try to navigate decisions and finances and duty."

—**Nicole Helget,** author of *Stillwater* and *The End of the Wild*

"Liz Fiedorow Sjaastad's compelling memoir will break your heart, then fill it full of her generosity of spirit. This author knows how to keep readers turning pages with the anguishing turns of her life story, offered with gentle humor and lyrical writing and, above all, compassion. I will be sure to keep an eye out for all she writes."

—**Kate St. Vincent Vogl,** author of *Lost & Found: A Memoir of Mothers*

"Being raised by a mother with untreated schizophrenia leaves children living in two worlds. They are worlds that collide: the reality the mother's illness creates, and that of the rest of the world. It's confusing, frightening, and disorienting. Liz Fiedorow Sjaastad's journey as such a child, chronicled in *You're Too Young to Understand*, underscores how children feel the burden of helping their parents.

In such circumstances, living a life of meaning and happiness can be a daunting task, and Sjaastad tells the story of how she captured and nurtured such a life—all the while trying to understand, navigate, and help her parents. Among the powerful and life-affirming things this story does is help readers separate the person from their illness. Discovering who her mother and father were—which was too often eclipsed by their illnesses of schizophrenia and alcoholism—made it possible for Sjaastad to care for her aging parents. And it is that task, understanding the humanity of our parents, that is the universal truth told in this powerful and moving memoir."

—**Xavier Amador, PhD,** author of the international bestseller *I Am Not Sick, I Don't Need Help!: How to Help Someone with Mental Illness Accept Treatment*

"A beautifully written story of a woman determined to break the patterns of silence and avoidance that shaped her childhood. In clear and eloquent prose, Liz Fiedorow Sjaastad gives us a vivid portrayal of the bafflement and fear of a young child grappling with her mother's mental illness, and then an unflinching look at what it means to caretake someone who refuses all care.

Through her writing, Sjaastad tries to unravel the mystery of her troubled parents' perplexing and enduring bond. Sometimes funny, sometimes heartbreaking, *You're Too Young To Understand* is also a story of powerful sibling solidarity—offering the possibility that even in the most troubled of families, one good sister may be enough. And that even without much in the way of a parental roadmap, we can still find our way to love and forgiveness."

—**Laura Flynn,** author of *Swallow the Ocean*

LIZ FIEDOROW SJAASTAD

You're Too Young to Understand

A MEMOIR

WISE INK

You're Too Young to Understand © copyright 2025 by Liz Fiedorow Sjaastad. All rights reserved. No part of this book may be reproduced in any form whatsoever, by photography or xerography or by any other means, by broadcast or transmission, by translation into any kind of language, nor by recording electronically or otherwise, without permission in writing from the author, except by a reviewer, who may quote brief passages in critical articles or reviews.

This is a creative nonfiction memoir. As such, it is based on the author's memories as to events and how they occurred. The author recognizes that characters described in this book may have memories of the events described that are different from her own. Extensive editorial precautions have been taken to ensure diligence to the factual accuracy. Many names and identifying details have been changed to protect their privacy.

ISBN 13: 978-1-63489-757-0
Library of Congress Catalog Number: 2024927006
Printed in the United States of America
First Printing: 2025
29 28 27 26 25   5 4 3 2 1

Cover design by Mimi Bark
Interior design by Vivian Steckline
Edited by Kristen Tatroe and ScriptAcuity
Proofread by Shari MacDonald Strong and Abbie Phelps
Production editing by Lindsay Bohls

Wise Ink
PO Box 580195
Minneapolis, MN 55458-0195
WiseInk.com

Wise Ink is a creative publishing agency for game-changers. Wise Ink authors uplift, inspire, and inform, and their titles support building a better and more equitable world. For more information, visit WiseInk.com.

To order, visit ItascaBooks.com or LizSjaastad.com. Reseller discounts available.

Contact Liz Fiedorow Sjaastad at LizSjaastad.com for speaking engagements, freelance writing projects, and interviews.

DEDICATION

FOR THOSE WORKING TO better the lives of families impacted by schizophrenia through improved diagnosis, treatments, laws, and support systems.

And for my mother, Cathryn.

"Some of my old memories feel trapped in amber in my brain, lucid and burning, while others are like the wing beat of a hummingbird, an intangible, ephemeral blur."

—**Mira Bartok,** *The Memory Palace*

"Memory for me poses a kind of crisis in representation. Where the desire to capture what really happened meets the desire to build a story that will help us get on with our lives."

—**Lidia Yuknavitch,** *Reading the Waves*

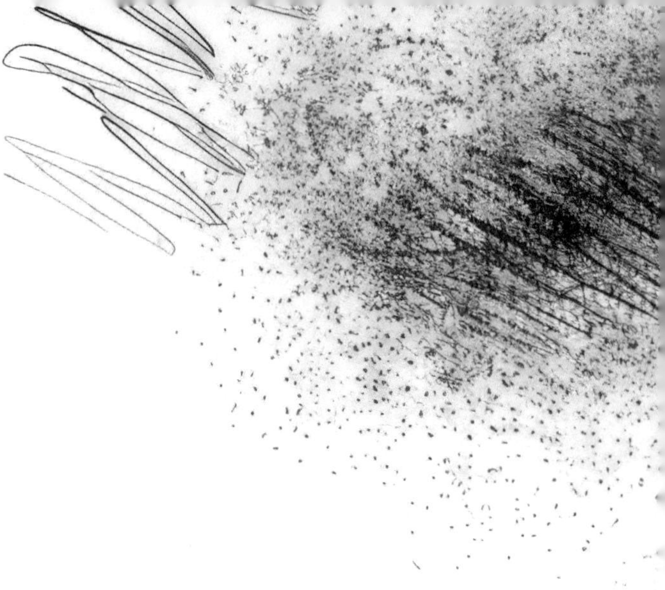

DAD'S FATE

MY OLDER SISTER KATE and I huddled outside the hospital meeting room. Our brother, Greg, had yet to arrive. Mom had already taken a seat inside the room by a picture window framing the Olympic Mountains. A pale mist veiled the dark forest.

In front of the mountain range, Mom ran through a repertoire of facial expressions like an actor preparing for an audition.

Kate's shoulders turned in, and she rubbed her hands. The pained look on her face told me her strength was waning.

"How should we do this?" I lifted my chin and eyebrows.

Kate took a deep breath. "We have to be sure Mom understands what Dad's life will be like, what her life will be like." She squatted and dropped her head between her knees, her hair hanging down. "How is this decision still hers?" she said from behind her hair curtain.

It'd been two weeks since Dad's massive brain bleed, and we were all on edge. Mom, on the verge of a breakdown, had been telling the nurses to put vitamin C and honey through Dad's IV if they wanted to save him, and we were still trying to reason with her, to reach a rational person we hoped still existed despite her illness.

I reached into my purse. "Here, take this." I extended my hand so Kate could see what I was offering. It was a Xanax a colleague had given me when I left town. Kate knew I had it, and though we were on either side of fifty, neither of us had ever taken one. The idea felt radical. She stood up, hesitated. Drugs and alcohol had ruined many in our family, yet Kate and I had escaped the darkness of addiction. She had escaped because of fear and thoughtful decision-making, and I had because . . . I don't know. Dumb luck, maybe?

"I'll take half." I broke the tiny white oval in two and put one of the halves on my tongue.

Kate's eyes lit up, and she put the pill in her mouth. We each swallowed our halves down without water and then side-smiled at each other. Mischievousness, a respite from crisis.

The doctor rushed past us and took a seat in the meeting room next to Mom. She had shoulder-length, black, wavy hair pulled back with a clip, and her full lips never moved to a smile. And why should they? What a terrible part of her job: talking with families as they decide when to let a loved one die.

Kate was stiff, her shoulders tight against her ears, making her neck look small. Sweat poured from my armpits, and I resisted the urge to let my mind wander to the mountain range. My pulse rose with the desire to release Kate from the burden of trying to enforce Dad's wishes, but neither of us really had any control. Mom was silent, her lips pursed, eyebrows narrowed. She moved around in her chair, trying to get comfortable as her brain likely told her what she'd already told us: that we should trust no one, that the doctors might be part of a grand plan to kill her husband.

Kate and I sat at the edges of our chairs, breathing intentionally, hoping for lucid Mom but fearing the alternative.

1

1

COUNTING TRAIN CARS

PRESIDENT NIXON RESIGNED a year after he told the country that he was not a crook or a quitter. Later in my life, I read that he might have suffered from paranoia and depression. But at age seven and in the second grade, I knew nothing about the Watergate scandal or mental illness. I had other pressing concerns: trains.

Our house on Fremont Street, in the small town of Galesburg, Illinois, was two blocks from a train crossing and two blocks from Silas Willard Elementary School, where I had to deal with the third-grade bullies, Jimmy and Joey. They chased me after school, once catching me and pushing my face into the wet snow. After tugging my pants down, they laughed and ran off. When Mom asked later what was the matter, I sobbed and whimpered but couldn't get the words out. I was worried she'd think I did something wrong. When I finally did tell her, she backed away and said, "Oh, that's it?" She didn't seem to think it was a big deal, which made me feel better, then worse.

I had first heard the loud train up close a couple of years earlier, when Mom and I were out walking our dog Tawny. As we neared the tracks, a train's horn blasted into what had been residential silence, sending me a foot off the ground in a jump scare. The jarring sound rattled my entire body. A giant beast of metal chugged hard and fast toward us, wheels screeching against rails. With a fear like I'd never known in my five years exploding inside me, I hightailed it straight for home. When I looked back, I saw Mom still in the same spot, slightly bent at the hips, laughing.

I feared the train's power as much as I did its earsplitting horn. A locomotive would smash anything it encountered, and the railroad system dominated our town. It had once provided an economic boom for Galesburg and was still essential to the local economy. As a result, a spiderweb of tracks spread through the area, and many of my classmates' families relied on railroad job income.

Once, dared by my brother Greg, I gently set a penny on the shiny metal track when we heard the roaring monster making its way toward us. I turned, and my pounding heart propelled me into the tall weeds of a ditch. I sat up fast and pressed my palms to my ears. The train thundered by, and vibrations from the rails passed through the earth to my butt and up to my throat. After the caboose was gone from sight, I clambered up the hill and grabbed the flattened copper. The hot metal burned my finger. I dropped the penny, looked back, and saw Greg standing by the sidewalk, bent at the hips, laughing.

· · • · ·

THE WINTER SKY WAS clear and the air crisp the day I rode alone with Mom to the League of Women Voters, where she volunteered. As we approached a set of train tracks, the safety bar lowered. I covered my ears for the brain-blasting horn. I'd heard the sound so many times by the age of seven that it didn't shake me up as much anymore.

Mom put the car in park, which was a bad sign.

"This looks like a long, slow one." She turned off the ignition. It could be twenty of the longest minutes of my life before we'd move again.

I was bored but didn't say so. I knew Mom's response to that statement. I'd heard it many times: *Only boring people get bored. Find something to do.* I huffed my discontent instead. She pointed to the train and moved her finger up and down as it went by. "Be patient, Liza. Count the freight cars. I'll bet there are at least a hundred!"

She had taught me to count to high numbers while waiting for the caboose. As I neared three hundred, the train slowed, then stopped, and started backing up.

"It's going backward!" I slumped further into my seat.

Mom focused on the rearview mirror, which she'd turned toward her. Taking small sections of her short brown hair into her first two fingers and her thumb, she moved them in a twisting motion to create waves. Then she pinched her cheeks and smacked her lips.

"Why'd you pinch your cheeks?"

"A lady doesn't need to wear rouge when her cheeks can be naturally rosy from a little pinch."

Mom spent a lot of time in front of the mirror at home, and Greg and Kate would laugh as they sang along to the lyrics of the song "You're So Vain" by Carly Simon. Mom laughed too but corrected them; she wasn't vain.

I didn't really know what it meant to be vain, but I put the pieces together. Mom thought it was important to look a certain way. She walked into rooms with her chin up, and she didn't seem to like people who didn't have their chins up too. I think sometimes that Dad tried to fit her mold of a chin-up professor. But he liked chatting with people who didn't care about appearing sophisticated.

Mom didn't think Kate was ladylike enough. She corrected Kate often for how she walked and talked. Whenever Mom had friends over in the town we'd lived in before Galesburg, she'd seemed embarrassed by Kate, especially if Kate said anything. Mostly we were supposed to stay upstairs and be quiet, neither seen nor heard.

Mom told me that in high school, she'd written for the newspaper and studied French. I once saw a photo from her student council days. In the picture, she sat with her knees together, ankles crossed under her full skirt, showing off a twenty-inch waist. Like a young Audrey Hepburn, her dark hair in a pixie cut, she sat, chin high, showing the length of her sleek neck. She seemed very ladylike and sophisticated.

Stuck in the car with Mom now, I pinched my cheeks then looked in the rearview mirror, smiled, and smacked my lips. My cheeks, called *gumball cheeks* by Dad, turned red. It worked!

I sighed. There was no other choice but to wait for the train. It was Galesburg, where no one was in a hurry and everybody seemed to know everybody—except us, of course, as we were new to town and my parents were slow to make friends.

Only one couple had visited our house so far. The husband, an arrogant but charismatic man, loved to cook Italian food. He smelled like garlic. The wife, an artistic woman who dressed in bold colors, spoke while holding her arms wide. She smelled like strawberries.

Soon after we moved to town, the four of them—Mom, Dad, Garlic, and Strawberry—walked through our house. Mom and Dad were giving the couple a tour with me tagging along. Mom moved her shoulders and hips more than usual as they walked down the stairs to our basement. They stopped to look at our Picasso print, the black-and-white Don Quixote. Strawberry knew a lot about the artwork and spoke about the skill and care that, although not obvious at first glance, Picasso had used to create the painting. Dad, with a slight smile, stood with them, but seemed separate. Garlic spoke with speed and authority about the hero represented in the artwork, adding while pushing out his chest that men like this man reach a point where they must pack up and leave, travel the world.

Mom listened to Garlic like I'd never seen her listen to anyone. Bright-eyed and attentive, she touched his arm and laughed. Dad, who'd been quiet—not seeming too interested—stepped farther back and lost his smile.

My stomach turned, and I rushed to Dad's side. He looked down at me. "Go outside and play, butterball." I looked down, pivoted, and made my way toward the stairs.

My parents' problems didn't begin here, but this event marks my first memory of my body telling me something my brain had yet to understand. It was also the last time that couple came to our home.

Sometimes Dad would try to outrun the train by driving down the streets to make it to the next crossing before the bars went down. With Mom, we counted train cars. There must be two types of people, I thought: the patient waiters and the impatient movers. I decided that if I could drive, I'd be a mover like Dad. I didn't yet know why, but being in motion seemed safer than sitting in one place tethered to Mom.

I looked out the car window as we waited for the train that was moving forward now. Century-old homes—some with peeling white, brown, and blue paint, broken windows, and sunken porches—lined the block.

I rolled down my window and smelled the air. From my nose to my throat, I tasted the acrid stuff that's used to treat the railroad ties. The cornfields began not far away and stretched to the end of the world. Trains could move for miles alongside black dirt tilled for crops without ever sounding their horns. I held that image and that silence in my head.

Mom saw me looking out the window and said, "Hon, we'll talk about this later at home, but I wanted to tell you we're moving to France this summer."

I swung my head around and met her eyes. She was smiling. Trying to understand what moving to France meant, I wondered if I'd get away from loud, long trains. And bully twins.

"Your father was picked to be the professor on-site in Besançon, France, for a year or two. You'll go to school there in the fall."

· · • · ·

A FEW WEEKS LATER, we were all in the car driving home from an event at Knox College when Dad pointed at the college president's home and said, "Guess what? We could have moved in there!"

"What? Really?" Open-mouthed, I admired the large, historic home at the corner of North Prairie and Losey Streets: yellow brick with yard enough for twenty croquet games. I imagined myself looking out one of the windows on the second floor, my bedroom window, down at the me who didn't live in the grand house.

Poker-faced, he said, "That's right. They offered me the job of president, but I turned it down. We're going to France instead."

Everyone laughed. I looked at my sister and brother with my mouth open again. Greg, three years older than I, and Kate, three years older than Greg, always got the jokes that I didn't. Mom attempted to hide a smile. I sat stunned—why was this funny?

It was a big deal, my family laughing together. The only other times we laughed together were when Tim Conway paired up with Harvey Korman on *The Carol Burnett Show* or when Edith slew Archie with an innocent one-liner. I liked it, and happy to have something to boast about, I later told several of my friends, including professors' daughters, that my dad could've been president, but he turned the offer down to go to France.

It was years before I found out Dad was joking. I believed everything he said back then; he was a professor, after all. He didn't talk a whole lot, but when he did, I listened, and I believed.

But they weren't joking about going to France. "It'll be an ideal time to immerse ourselves, our family, in the culture and the language," my parents told us at the dinner table.

"What a great opportunity!" Mom beamed at Dad, and he returned a rare smile.

None of it made sense. I was only seven, but I recognized that when my parents smiled at each other it was a special thing. They weren't a happy couple, and they fought a lot, but they were happy with the idea of moving to France, and that made the move good for me. I didn't mind leaving Galesburg, its garlic-smelling man, its trains, and its bully twins.

2

FRANCE

ONE DAY, BEFORE OUR move to France, Kate kneeled, Greg reclined, and I sat cross-legged on the floor, all of us on the same side of the coffee table. Kate's long hair, the color of pale-yellow corn, was parted in the middle. It was so dirty it looked greasy, as was often the case. Mom and Dad only let us bathe once a week, and she had oilier skin than Greg and I did. When her hair was clean, it shone like a star and felt like silk, and I wished it were mine.

Tawny lay cross-pawed next to me, her nose resting on the floor. She glanced up at Mom, who sat on the edge of our mustard-colored couch. Tawny's eyebrow ridges switched directions when she looked at me as if checking on me.

Mom, in teacher mode—ready to educate us like she did her high school French students—placed flash cards on the table and told us to repeat after her. "*Ou est le WC?*" Translated: "Where is the restroom?" "*Je parle un petit peu français.*" Translated: "I speak a little bit of French."

I did my best to mimic her. Getting the accent right was important to

Mom. But we weren't her high school students. I was seven, Greg ten, and Kate thirteen.

Mom was the younger of two kids in her family. She and her sister, Carol, had grown up in Seattle. My grandpa Howard, a stoic or maybe just an insensitive Norwegian, had kept to his routines and pinched his pennies. Grandma Florence, born in England, had been quick to laugh despite being a refined Brit. She died young from vascular dementia when I was in elementary school. She'd passed along her English etiquette and sometimes-haughty demeanor to her daughters—my aunt Carol and my mom, Cathy—who'd attempted, and failed, to mold their squirrelly American children into British-mannered tots. Teaching us French wasn't proving to be any easier.

"No. Listen to the accent: *Je parle*. Can you hear the *r*? It comes from constricting the back of your throat. Try making the *r* sound." Mom sighed.

Greg, the only blue-eyed, dimpled person in our family, acted feral. He jumped up and made the sound. "It's like you're about to hock a loogie!"

Mom's face brightened. She chuckled. "That's right."

Kate and I imitated Greg in our effort to become good French speakers. The sound of all three of us kids preparing to hock loogies, cracking up the whole time, got Tawny, who was now standing, more interested too. I was going to miss Tawny, but I was comforted by Mom telling us she'd be well taken care of by the people who would be staying in our home while we were gone.

Unable to get us to focus again, Mom ended our lesson. Having equipped us with the *r* sound and the ability to find the potty, she'd prepared us to live abroad for a year.

Mom hoped we'd all learn to speak French like the French do. Not like Americans who try to speak French but can never get the accent right. "Appalling!" she'd said. Before we left Galesburg, I practiced. I took a breath to gather my nerve and said, "*Je m'appelle Liza. J'ai sept ans.*"

Meaning, my name is Liza. I'm seven years old. I looked at Mom for approval. She repeated what I'd said in a beautiful and animated French accent. She was as flawless as a mannequin in a department store. And just as hard to hug.

In late spring of 1975, the Fiedorow five—"I *feed-a-row* of children," Dad said to help people pronounce the American version of our last name, Fyoderov—left our small, wood-sided home near the train tracks and flew across the sea to the city of Besançon, France.

The city, built along the meander of the river Doubs, sits at the edge of the Jura Mountains. The grungy gray building we lived in, which connected to several other gray stone buildings, was in the square called Place de Lattre de Tassigny. *Place de Lattre de Tassigny* was fun to say and sounded strange. Very French. Nothing like *Fremont Street*.

To get to our small second-floor apartment, we traveled a narrow, dark stairway between a mechanic's garage on one side and a diner on the other. The entire time we were abroad, I choked on diesel exhaust while inhaling the sweet smells of baked pastries.

We arrived in France at the beginning of summer, and my siblings and I attended an outdoor day camp. My group was the orange group. When it was time for us to gather, a counselor would scream, "*Lesssss Oraaaaannges!*" Alone in Les Oranges group with the French kids, I was a Martian. I had nothing in common with the Earthlings, and my "*Ou est le WC?*" didn't win me new friends. I picked up a nervous habit of licking my fingertips whenever they started feeling desert dry, intensifying the fingertip drought.

I clung to a camper my age named Marianne. My human security blanket had a heart-shaped face squared off at the top by chocolate-brown bangs. She didn't shake me off like the others, who preferred not to play with the weird foreign girl who licked her fingertips.

Whenever I was offered the option to nap, I panicked. What if I woke and Marianne was gone? To me, the camp was as big as the country. If

Marianne wanted to rest, I'd say I did too, and I'd stay awake until rest time was over. I spent each day this way, an American Martian in France.

Across the street and down the road from our apartment, a stone stairway led up the side of the mountain range to the Citadel of Besançon. Previously used in many battles, the stone structure was now a zoo and Holocaust museum.

One sunny weekend afternoon, after a week at camp, Kate, Greg, and I climbed the mountain stairs to spend time at the zoo. We fed peanuts to chimpanzees named Belle and Boy, a pair we connected with. They'd come close to the bars, stick their arms through, show us their palms, and knock their knuckles on the platform that separated us to tell us they wanted more peanuts. We looked into their eyes. They looked into ours.

Hot and hungry, Greg and I started picking at each other. To get away from him, I wandered toward the stone arch entrance to the museum. Standing between the stone building and the chimpanzees, I licked my fingertips and glanced back to be sure Kate and Greg weren't looking for me. Kate sat hunched on a bench reading, her hair in her face. Greg shook his bag of peanuts wildly, trying to lure Belle and Boy. Belle and Boy, having grown tired of begging, lazed behind their bars and allowed flies to gather.

The tunnel to the museum was cool and damp, inviting, and though I could read the sign prohibiting children from entering without adults, I kept walking. I tiptoed into a quiet, cold room and rubbed my goose-bumped arms. It took a minute for my eyes to adjust to the darkness. The room was black, punctuated by beams of light that shone on framed black-and-white photographs lining the walls. I peered over my shoulder. No one was around. I moved closer to the pictures, then stopped short. A large mound of naked bodies with limp arms and legs, with torsos that were all hip, rib, and collarbones: a two-story high pile of dead, skin-and-bone humans. My head spun. As I turned to run, I lost my balance and fell to the floor. I pulled myself up and ran out of the room, through the damp tunnel, into the bright daylight.

I was still only seven, but I knew people didn't get that way in one day. Those people had had it worse than animals in cages at the zoo. They'd starved before their bodies were thrown into piles, like garbage. Who did this to them and why?

Scattered and scared, I ran back to Belle and Boy. I sat by their concrete cage, looked into their eyes, and saw a sadness I hadn't seen before. Kate and Greg slouched on the bench, unaware I'd been gone. I'd seen something I wasn't supposed to see, that I couldn't understand, I knew that much. My fingertips were dry but also tingling, and before I could lick them, the zoo began to spin.

I stood up slowly, wobbled my way to the bench, and scooted in between Kate and Greg. I squeezed my eyes shut and tried to will away visions of dead bodies.

· · • · ·

IN THE AUTUMN OF our year in France, on the first day of school at L'École Victor Hugo, the kids asked, while pointing at me, "*C'est une fille ou un garçon?*" Meaning, "Is it a girl or a boy?" This, I suspected, was not a good start, particularly at a girls' school.

I tried to disappear at my desk. I didn't understand the language, but the teachers paddled children who answered questions wrong, and they paddled even harder if the children broke rules. After establishing my gender, I set out to avoid the paddle. In fact, I pretty much just sat, head down, frozen in fear.

Kate, at a different school, was in a class with kids younger than her, and the boys there teased her. She found a security blanket of her own, a strong-willed girl named Beatrice who stood up to the mean boys and shielded Kate. Despite feeling awkward and shy, she did well in school and learned French, though, like me, she preferred not to speak it.

Greg's teachers summoned misbehaving children to their desks and told them to hold the palms of their hands up and place their fingertips together. The teachers then whacked, with a long, wooden stick, the tips of those fingers, hitting the nerve endings. These stories scared my fingertip-licking self, and Greg fell in line while at school.

Greg made friends and was comfortable speaking French. In front of his new neighborhood pals, he showed off and made fun of Kate, who kept to herself with her head in a book.

Kate had begun having trouble sleeping around the time she first heard Mom and Dad fighting at night back in Galesburg. Fearful of the anger and shouting, she hid cotton balls under her pillow, wishing that, in her ears, they'd mute the shouting. By the time we lived in France, Kate was sleeping only every other night. Anxiety would keep her awake one night, and the next night, she'd collapse with exhaustion. With dark circles under her eyes and slumped shoulders, she walked around in a daze. She told me she liked the dulled-senses feeling she had the day after not sleeping. In France, to get away from the tension and anger that were now confined to a tiny apartment, she went for hours-long walks by herself in the foreign city. She took the bus to her tennis lessons, escaping and hoping the exercise would help with her feelings of nighttime panic and insomnia.

Greg told me that when we got back to the United States, I'd flunk out of school for not knowing my multiplication tables. For this, and for other unknown reasons, I cried often. Not just tears but body-heaving sobs and wails. Greg called me the "the Waterworks" and made it his mission to make me cry daily. I consistently failed at my daily mission not to.

He made up a song about me and sang it over and over until it sounded in my head long after he moved on: "Little Liza cries all the time! Little Liza doesn't know why!" I cried louder, hoping to get Mom's attention. Exhausted, she'd yell at me, "Enough already, Liza! Stop that crying!"

Living on the river Doubs in the summer meant hot, humid nights and armies of massive, thirsty mosquitoes. Our apartment's windows had shutters with no screens, but it was hot and Greg and I needed fresh air, so we kept our shutters open. I pulled my knees to my chest and yanked my shirt over my head for protection against the bloodsuckers that were hovering, then charging into my skin.

Greg marched in with two rolled-up newspapers. "We can take 'em! Here!" He shoved a weapon into my hands. I gleefully accepted.

We bounced on the beds and lunged at the walls with our newspapers. We refused to go to sleep until they were all smashed dead. I was convinced they wanted *my* blood; the nickel- and dime-size red welts covering my cheeks proved it. Dad said they chose me because I was sweet. Yet armed with rolled-up newspapers, Greg and not-so-sweet me whacked the walls, high-fived each other's kills, and celebrated the blood splotches when we were done. Our blood, from their squashed bodies, marked the beige walls and proved us victorious.

Our family attended operas, operettas, plays, and musicals. The performances were not in English, but in many ways, I liked the nights out of the apartment. I wore my fanciest Mom-made dress and acted quiet and proper like Mom wanted. When I got upset, as I did regularly in France, I tried hard to keep my tears inside and my fingertip-licking to a minimum, sitting on my hands if necessary.

Most of the time, Dad was out of the apartment until late at night. When he was home, often working at his desk in the living room, we were to be quiet. He and Mom both tried to enforce this rule, but we were kids, and Greg had too much energy, not enough space, and not enough focus.

One night after dinner, Greg jumped around like a monkey, hunched over, swinging his arms, making faces at me. At first, it was fun, and I laughed at him. Then he kept at it even when I tried to get away from him.

"Stop it!" I screamed.

"Oo oo ah ah! Oo oo ah ah!" His face was in mine, his arms sweeping about.

I ran. "Stay away!"

Wherever I hid, he found me. I sneaked into Kate's room directly across the hall from ours, and he followed me.

"Get out of my room!" Kate yelled.

I ran to our room, and he was in my face within a second. I started running faster between the rooms and slamming the door each time. Slam. Run. Slam. Run. Slam. Run. Slam.

Dad came out of nowhere when I was in our room hiding, picked me up by the waist like a rag doll, held me over my bed, and spanked me hard. Three hard swats. He put a lot of effort into those hits, not like the random smacks on the leg or bottom he or Mom had given before. After the three hard belts, he let go and dropped me three feet to my bed, and I cried myself to sleep.

My eyes were still red and swollen from crying when I joined everyone the next morning at the round little kitchen table. Kate, Greg, and I all reached for the comics section of the newspaper at the same time, a regular fight for us. Dad beat us to it, and with his large, thick, cigarette-stained fingers, he folded the comics section and gently handed it to me, saying, "Liza gets it first." I knew it was because he felt guilty; favoring someone was one way he apologized for his bad behavior. It wasn't because he liked me most, but I let myself think that, and I took the prize anyway.

· · • · ·

I DIDN'T KNOW THEN that when my dad had been my age, seven, he was in Europe during World War II and saw plenty of dead bodies in real life.

There was no consensus as to the date and year of Dad's, Vasily's, birth. As the oldest of three brothers born in Russia to Gregory and Olga, his birth occurred in September, on either the fourth or the ninth in either 1938 or 1939. Family lore was that Olga, my Nana, changed his birthdate when it meant extra food rations and had then forgotten the real year.

Before my dad was born, millions of previously prosperous land-owning peasants were starving during collectivism policy that involved taking land, food, and equipment from farmers. During this time Nana ate rats to survive, and her yet-to-be husband, Gregory, a teenager, was sent to a prison work camp for six years when he tried to defend his family's property from confiscation by the government.

My grandpa never had an alliance to the government that imprisoned him for defending his family's business, so after Germany invaded Russia, he fought for whoever would pay him. Meanwhile, my grandma Olga and her boys fled from one bombed village to another. Dad, four or five years old, remembers flying shattered glass, ear-blasting explosives, a pillow over his head. Then the Germans forced his family onto a train in a boxcar meant for animals and cargo. The doors slammed shut and the train rumbled away from bucolic Russia. That train moved people one direction only. Dad wouldn't see his hometown again for forty-eight years.

When the war ended, after Dad had spent years as a child in a prison work camp in Germany, the Allied forces liberated his family and relocated them to a displaced persons camp. In April 1945, at the age of seven or eight, my dad stood on the dirt road at the refugee camp and watched as soldiers forced his father onto a truck that would take him away from his family forever.

At that time, there was a secret postwar agreement between the US, Britain, and Russia, made at Stalin's request, to exclude soldiers from Russia from the option to relocate to other welcoming countries. The grandpa I'd never meet was sent to Siberia for fifteen years' hard labor and exile. He lived the rest of his life there, never seeing his wife and sons again.

In June 1947, while still in the refugee camp with her sons, Dad's mom, my nana, remarried a short and stern Russian named Serge. My grandparents were not likely legally divorced before Nana's second marriage. It was wartime; perhaps this didn't matter so much.

Serge relocated to Belgium from the refugee camp to start work as a coal miner. Shortly afterward, he wrote to Nana to tell her not to come, saying that he had changed his mind about marriage and raising her three sons. Nana, headstrong and determined, went anyway in October 1947.

Serge became an abusive stepfather to Dad. Dad, living with the stepfather who did not want him, attended school for the first time in Belgium at age eight. He discovered a love for languages and learning. He devoured books as quickly as he devoured Nana's beet-based borscht.

· · • · ·

DAD CAME INTO OUR living room in France and sat down next to me as I watched TV. He put his arm around my whole body and pulled me up against him for a nice side hug. "How's my little butterball with the knobby knees?" he asked.

I melted in his embrace, then looked at Kate and Greg. I was sure that they wished they had his attention, because I always wanted it when they had it.

Kate was Dad's favorite. Dad said Kate could be anything she wanted to be, including a medical doctor. Yet, in France, Kate was privy to his dark side too. She experienced his quakes while I absorbed the aftershocks.

One night, at an Italian restaurant where we were eating with Dad's students, an inch-long canker sore under my front bottom teeth kept me from eating the tomato-sauced foods. I watched the adults and grimaced instead. By the third course, Mom had fixed her attention on a male student of Dad's who was telling stories. Mom focused her gaze, changed her posture, and tilted her head. Her flirting was Jane Austen–like, an old-school English style of flirting. The young man seemed the only person in the room who mattered to her. She laughed her exaggerated laugh at his jokes while Dad lit one cigarette after another, drank, and withdrew.

After dinner, Dad stayed out, and Mom, Kate, Greg, and I came home. Mom went straight to the bathroom.

Kate peeked down the hallway before grabbing an open bottle of wine. She whispered to Greg and me, "Keep watch."

Greg nodded, and Kate, with her hand shaking, poured almost all the wine out into the kitchen sink. Then Greg went to the living room and grabbed a half-empty bottle of vodka and brought it back to the kitchen. He positioned it below the faucet and diluted it with water before placing it back where he found it.

Didn't matter. Late that night, Dad roared from the kitchen, "Where are you, Cathy?"

He lurched past Kate, who was peeking out her bedroom door toward the living room. Mom, tucked into the fold-out couch that was her and Dad's bed, stayed silent.

"I know you're awake. Get up, you whore!" He yanked open the closet door, grabbed a suitcase, and threw it on the bed. "Why don' you jus' pack up, and get da hell outta here? You don' wanna be here, and I don' wan' you here!" He was yelling, Russian accent heavy with liquor, slurring his words.

Kate snagged her ruffled nightgown on the doorjamb as she went to Mom's rescue. She grabbed Mom, pulled her into her bedroom, and slammed the door. It sounded like they barricaded the door with furniture to keep him out.

Dad pounded on the bedroom door. "Let me in! Cathy, you get out here! You wan' out of dis goddamned apartment, dis marriage? You should leave already! I have a suitcase for you. Go find someone better."

Mom eventually came out of the room to try to calm Dad down. They argued until Mom passed out from exhaustion on the hallway floor.

Kate watched in horror as Dad stepped over Mom to get to the bathroom. "How can you just step over her like that?" she screamed. "Aren't you at all worried about her—don't you care?"

He didn't respond.

Mom and Kate never spoke about these nights. But after his bouts of drunken behavior, Dad took Kate on walks during which he'd plead for forgiveness and apologize. He promised it would never happen again, he would stop drinking. Kate, barely a teenager, carried the weight, the confusion, the anxiety of that promise. Had he promised Mom or anyone else that he'd quit? Likely, he'd promised Mom. He didn't quit, though—he drank.

Some weeks later, I sat on our couch in the small living room and watched a children's animated show called *Filopat et Patafil*. Filopat and Patafil were rubbery stick figures with wooden balls for heads, black painted dots for eyes, and wooden noses. They didn't speak; they had no mouths. They were expressionless, their stories told through body movements, music, a few simple props.

Knees to my chest, holding my shins, I brought all ten fingertips to my mouth. I stuck out my tongue and wet them before the sensation of throbbing dryness drove me crazy.

Bored with the show, I eyed my mom's Ansco Shur Shot box camera. When cupped in my hands, the camera—a five-by-seven-inch box covered in textured, black faux leather with silver edges—gave me purpose and a feeling of control over my world. Mom sometimes gave me the camera just to use. I wanted it to be mine. The black strap around my neck held it securely at my waist. I looked through it from above to take pictures, to frame the world as I saw it, to frame the world as I wanted it to be. I took it out when we went to the zoo, to Paris, and to the corner store.

My stomach grumbled. I left Filopat and Patafil and walked into the kitchen. Mom stood with her back to me, smoking a cigarette near the window next to the adjacent wall that held the small refrigerator, an old stove, and a farmhouse sink.

I stood for a moment in the kitchen. I'd have to interrupt the silence to get her attention. I swallowed, considered speaking French, but changed my mind. "I'm hungry." I waited for her to sing, "*En français?*"

She looked through me before turning back to the window. "We'll be eating soon. Why don't you take this to the corner store and buy a baguette for our lunch?" She handed me a franc from her pocket without removing her gaze from the street. The corner store, visible from our apartment windows, was a short walk, but I was hesitant to go it alone and have to ask for the baguette in French. I thought of the camera. I took the money from Mom and grabbed the Shur Shot on my way out.

I wondered what was so important out the window. She couldn't see the mechanic's garage below our apartment or the restaurant next door. Maybe it was the pale-green buds on the few trees that lined the street across from the parking lot—its pavement glistening after an early-morning rain or the customary washing of sidewalks that cleaned away the dirt and dog pee from the day before. I thought of Tawny, back in America, always peeing in the grass outside our home, and wondered if she would feel comfortable peeing on stone. I missed Tawny. Maybe Mom did too. Tawny and I had our own language, which we spoke with our eyes. I'd lie on my stomach in front of her, our noses almost touching, and share my deepest seven-year-old thoughts by thinking them into her round, brown eyes. She'd tell me everything was going to be all right and that she understood.

Diesel exhaust, sewage, and bakery items. The smells of my French city were different, and I longed for the familiar odors of home: sweet-smelling grass, pungent railroad ties, even manure from farms nearby. On my way home, feeling confident after having spoken French and buying the bread, I reached into the brown paper bag and tore off the top of the warm baguette. The crispy crust crunched against my teeth, and the moist middle melted on my tongue. I dug my fingers in deeper for more.

I zigzagged by the diner next to our apartment, hoping to see Valerie and Corrine, two girls I played with sometimes. Their parents owned the restaurant, and we'd often jump rope together just outside the diner door. I caught a glimpse of their mom. She was holding up her skirt with her teeth, like she always did when she pulled up her nylons. That way, she could use both hands on one leg at a time to get those nylons up. I'd never in my life seen my mom do something like that. I'm sure I hadn't even seen my mom's underwear. I considered taking a picture, capturing the image of a soft mom, but I quickly looked down and made the turn up the narrow, dark stairway to our apartment.

I placed the torn loaf of bread on our laminated kitchen table and licked my fingertips. I was in luck: Mom still seemed distracted, so much so that she didn't notice the bread I'd already started to eat. She was facing the sink now instead of the window, her hip resting on the counter, another cigarette in hand.

Before I could leave the room, she said, "Did you see all of them?"

"Who?" I asked.

"The women outside, the ones dressed like me. Their hair is exactly like mine." She touched her hair for emphasis. "That's peculiar, don't you think?" It was a demand, not a question.

I examined her navy skirt, her white blouse—what was she talking about? I licked my fingertips again, as they had gotten very dry, then shrugged. "I didn't see them."

Mom waited. Weariness washed over her face before anger wrenched the sides of her mouth and she raised her chin. "You must not have been looking. There were dozens of them, looking just like me, standing just below the apartment."

A small part of me wanted to say I thought *she* was the one that was peculiar, but a bigger part wondered how I'd missed all those women dressed like her. Where could they have been? My educated mother was smart and always acted like she was a whole level above the rest of us. Her superiority wafted around her like a perfume. At that time, if she said she saw the women, I didn't doubt that she did.

I regretted not taking a picture of Valerie and Corrine's mom, and maybe of the shiny sidewalks that reminded me of Tawny back in the US. I went back to watching *Patafil et Filopat*, pulled my knees to my chest, and held on to myself.

A MONTH OR SO later, I skip-walked my usual route home from school, moving in and out of the concrete gutter that separated the road from the sidewalk. We'd been in France for just under a year, and Mom had gone to Spain to travel with her sister, Carol. Dad had become an attentive parent, cooking silly, kid-friendly meals, vacuuming, dusting, and generally hanging out with us. He stayed home at night, but he spent hours gazing out the kitchen window.

The sweet smells of freshly baked *pain au chocolat* and éclair pastries swirled in the air as I made my way home through the brick-and-stone city, swerving around people, hopping into the street gutter and out again. I arrived at our street, peeked in Valerie and Corrine's family's restaurant, and then climbed the narrow, wet-stone-scented stairway to our apartment.

I opened the door to find Mom, Aunt Carol, and Mom's aunt and uncle—my Great-Aunt Hilda and Great-Uncle Ivan—in the kitchen. Surprised, I hugged our visitors and then looked at Mom for answers. She sat at the kitchen table, her forehead leaning on her hand. Her face was red and swollen from crying.

Aunt Carol stepped back and put me at arm's length. "We are here, Liza, to take you, your mom, Katie, and Greg back to the United States. We are leaving for the Paris airport today!" She forced a smile.

I wanted to be excited to go home, but Mom was upset. Aunt Hilda put her soft arm around me and ushered me out of the kitchen. "We packed you up, dear, but go make sure we've gotten everything."

In the living room, Dad pleaded with Kate, "Please stay with me. Don't go!" Kate cried and Dad begged some more. I didn't get why Mom, Dad, and Kate were so upset. I thought that we all wanted to go back home and that Dad only had to stay the extra two months until the end of his one-year commitment. It didn't occur to me that Mom was leaving Dad and Dad had already pleaded with her.

In our room, Greg's grin covered his face. "We're going home, Waterworks! We'll get to see Tawny!"

The next day in a hotel room in Paris, the day before our big flight across the ocean, Greg taunted me again about not knowing my multiplication tables. I didn't cry, because Kate and Mom were still crying, and it was all too much. Uncle Ivan—a tall, bald Swede, and the kindest man I knew—helped me make a plan to study on the plane. I'd make flash cards and quiz myself until I had them all memorized.

But no one could help my big sister. Aunt Carol took Kate into the bathroom and scolded her. "Stop crying already," she said. "You're just making it worse for your mom!"

3

SEATTLE WITH FAMILY

UNCLE IVAN AND AUNTS Hilda and Carol swooped in, opened their wings, and held Mom close as we flew from France without Dad. I see now that they were focused on saving Mom from her husband, and this was perhaps why no one seemed to notice how her brain had changed.

On the plane ride home, I studied my multiplication tables and licked my fingertips in the dry airplane air. I was excited to go back to America, back to see Tawny! Mom, her nose red and her eyes puffy, clutched an embroidered handkerchief. Kate quietly wrote in her lock-and-key journal while Greg played like he was vomiting into the barf bag.

I don't remember being worried about Dad.

I could picture him on the day after we left without him. In my mind, like on any other day after work, or after drinking, he climbed the dark and narrow stairway, briefcase in hand, and opened the door to the apartment to find it empty. He set his briefcase down, the metal knobs on the bottom making a tapping sound as they landed on the table. The sound bounced off the walls and announced, "They're gone!" As he walked through the rooms, he noticed they appeared free of clutter.

When he took a deep breath, the air smelled of Aunt Hilda's perfume and our quick exit.

Ten years later, I'd find out what really happened to Dad after we left.

The rest of us flew from Paris, France, to Seattle, Washington. We arrived at my cousins' house in the University District of Seattle, and pandemonium immediately set in. Kate and I were okay, but Greg couldn't stop torturing our fiery middle cousin, Gina, who never failed to rise to his bait.

I overheard Aunt Carol and Uncle Cass talking. "Damn it, Carol, how can I get any work done here with three extra kids free roaming and fighting in the house? I've got papers to grade and deadlines."

"Cass, this is family. This is Cathy, my only sister, and her kids, and they've been through a tough time."

"How long? Can you tell me that? How long will they stay?"

"Shhhhhh! They're going to hear you," she said, adding, "I don't know. As long as they need to."

Our family settled in, trying our best to fit into the crowded two-story bungalow. Carol and Uncle Cass had three girls, the only cousins we knew. We'd go to their schools for the rest of the spring semester. Carla and I were close in age, seven and eight, respectively. We walked the three blocks to elementary school together after exiting her house through the back gate, the woodsy tang of pines and evergreen holly bushes guiding us down the alley. We often stopped to play at a large playground across from a Jack in the Box fast-food restaurant, on a cedar structure that lined the fence by her school.

Aunt Carol and Mom carried themselves spines straight, noses up. They tilted their heads, laughing, never taking us kids seriously. Their given names were Cathryn and Carol Rice, and besides their haughtiness, the biggest thing they had in common was what their daughters grew to call the Rice Sisters' Power of Denial. With this power, they could erase any undesirable thing from their lives by simply not acknowledging it. They denied illnesses and shortcomings that were right in front of them. They also had the power to tell you what you liked and didn't like, even if the issue was clearly a matter of personal taste.

Our cousins' family was never the same after our stay. I learned later in life that Carol and Cass had already been on shaky ground; our presence was the final rip in the fabric of their marriage. They divorced the following year.

Two months after we left France, we had a visit with Dad in Seattle. He looked different—much thinner, seemingly taller—and I could see his facial structure, his jawbone, the rugged hollow of his cheeks.

"How's my little butterball with the knobby knees?" he asked. The thinness made his smile cover the entire lower half of his face, like a clown's.

I looked down. "Good," I answered as if to a stranger.

He brought us toys. As he handed them out, he knelt, kept smiling this big smile, asked if we wanted to play a game with him. Unlike the hand-carved wooden figurines he'd buy on his annual trips to the Soviet Union for the college, these were manufactured toys, toys American kids would enjoy. The toys lifted my heart a bit, but the changes in Dad made my stomach hurt, and I licked my fingertips.

A week or so later, Carla and I sat on top of the monkey bars in her family's postage-stamp-size backyard. Carla was a true tomboy, and I envied that about her. Athletic, with a quiet confidence, she spoke through her clenched jaw using just her lips. She scratched at her knees, which were red and blotchy from allergies. Her long, dark-blond bangs fell in front of her face, down to her nose, and she left them there, shaking them back down whenever Aunt Carol brushed them aside.

We moved to a position where we hung by our knees and faced each other upside down.

"I have to go see a counselor with my family today," I said, having no idea what that meant.

"Oh, we've done that before." Carla was either confiding, bragging, or lying. She likely knew what counseling was and the reason we were going, a lot more than I did.

"Yeah. What happened?"

"Not much."

     · · ● · ·

ON THE WAY TO the therapy session in downtown Seattle, I looked out the back window and admired the city, the mountains, the waterfront. The sun was shining, the sky blue.

The three of us kids sat silently, and I focused on the Space Needle, with its futuristic shape and its spaceship restaurant at the top. I waited for Mom to say, "Look at the Space Needle, kids!" like she always did. She didn't. She told us that Carol had recommended this counselor and that we should all be on our best behavior. I thought she wanted us to behave because Carol had referred the counselor, not because it was important to our family's future.

First, Mom and Dad were in with the counselor with the door closed. We waited outside where there were *Highlights* magazines for us to look at. Kate had her book. After a long, quiet wait, the counselor opened the door and asked us to join the meeting.

In the counselor's office, I kept my knees together and my hands on my lap like Mom would want. Greg fidgeted in a chair next to me. He had tired, puffy eyes and messy hair. Kate pushed her glasses up her nose and sat waiting. I imagined that was how she looked in school, sitting at the front of the class. Mom and Dad sat next to each other but separate and stiff, like each of them was sitting next to someone who had the flu.

From a chair across the room, the family counselor sighed and slapped his palms on his lap. "Okay. Thanks for being here. I'm going to ask you some questions, and I hope we are able to talk today about how you all feel about living together again."

I side-looked at Dad. With clear eyes, dressed in new clothing that fit his thinner body, he sat up straight. Mom crossed her legs away from him.

The counselor asked Kate, "Did you have a happy childhood?"

Mom jumped in. "Of course she did!"

Kate nodded. It was too late for an honest answer.

He asked me, "Do you want your father to live with you again?"

I hesitated. A simple question, but our situation was complicated. Would he be wearing that weird smile again? Would he have more presents for us? The presents I liked, but the feeling that came with them I didn't. I told them what I thought they wanted to hear. "Yes, I think so."

My faced burned from having to speak at all. I couldn't look at Dad again, but, from the corner of my eye, I saw him sink back into his chair.

Our family pretended its way through the meeting. No one told the truth, not fully, but we all "behaved." No one said, "Dad drinks too much and gets mean, Mom no longer makes sense much of the time, and the kids are suffering and probably shouldn't be in this therapy session."

Before we left Seattle, Dad agreed to get help for his alcoholism, and he and Mom agreed to make a go of it again. We started life once more in a Galesburg that was much as we'd left it a year earlier. We moved back into the house on Fremont Street, near the train tracks and cornfields. I don't remember how it felt to see Tawny again after that year. Was she excited to see us? I'd missed Tawny more than our home, our street, and the grassy lawns. Yet when we finally came home, together as a family, I don't remember how Tawny greeted us or if I was happy. Maybe she wagged her tail and barked her greeting. Maybe I hugged her and told her how much I'd missed our conversations and our staring contests when I'd put my head down in front of hers and tell her my secrets. Maybe she didn't remember us because we'd been gone so long. It was a long time in dog years.

4

FLIGHT POTENTIAL

IT WAS BETTER TO expect the bad things and have my expectations met. I wouldn't have been able to articulate my feelings that way when I was nine, but that's when I started a life of low-expectation thinking.

The positive things in my life, the solidly good things that I could safely look forward to, were hanging out with my friend Heidi and procuring candy in any way possible. I'd search my parents' pockets for spare change and then walk the few blocks to buy the largest candy bar for the lowest price: the chocolate Charleston Chew.

When Heidi came over, we would run down to my musty, unfinished basement to distance ourselves from Greg, who always ruined our fun with teasing. We sat on the cool concrete floor and ate our candy. I tried nibbling some chocolate off my Charleston Chew before grabbing it with my molars and pulling hard as it stretched out six inches before breaking off. Our next order of business was acting out scenes from *Little House on the Prairie*. I was Laura, and Heidi was Mary.

One day, Greg found us in the basement. From behind the furnace, we heard him imitate us in a high-pitched voice, "Oh, Mary! Why are you so much prettier than me?"

"Shut up, Greg! Leave us alone!" My chin quivered.

He came out from hiding and squared off in front of me.

"Hey, funny face! Why don't you cry? Because, when you cry, your face looks like this." He made a face that did look a bit like mine when I cried. I knew this because I'd looked at myself in the mirror while crying after he made the face the first time.

He teased me about how my top lip covered my teeth and lower lip as it formed into a tight pointed *V* in the middle. The mirror had validated his tormenting claims.

Then he made fun of Heidi's short haircut, freckles, and clothes. He told us dirty jokes we didn't want to hear. I took her hand and led her upstairs to different rooms so we could put a door between him and us. He pinballed around the house after us. Fed up, Heidi got on her bike and rode home.

After she left, Greg taunted, bobbed, and weaved into the kitchen and backed me into the sink. I reached onto the countertop and grabbed a knife. A straight-edged knife, used for cutting raw meat or chopping vegetables, it was one of the knives regularly sharpened to make slicing and dicing a breeze. I held it in front of me in self-defense.

He backed away. "You won't do it. You won't use that knife. What are you going to do? Throw it at me? You're too chicken. You're a chicken and a crybaby with a funny lip!"

I couldn't stand it another moment. My mind and body bursting with anger, I whipped the knife at him. It was like the knife had a mind of its own.

Frantic, high-speed action switched into slow motion once the knife left my hand. I stared at Greg in horror and watched his gaze move downward from my hand. We both followed the trajectory of the knife until it pierced a half inch into his leg, near his shin, and stuck there. A dart in a dartboard.

With a calm that was strange for a twelve-year-old with a knife in his leg, he bent over, wrapped his hand around the knife handle, and tugged. He slid the knife from the raw meat of his shin. Frozen in terror, I expected retaliation and an uncontrollable anger to match my own.

"I can't believe you threw it."

I started crying again, panicked. "Please, I'm sorry! I didn't mean to!"

"I won't tell Mom. This would kill her. This is our secret," said the hero. His eyes glimmered.

He held the incident over my head for months.

"Lend me some money or I'll tell Mom about the knife!" He'd push me out of a seat and say, "Move or I'll tell Mom you tried to kill me with that knife!"

I gave him my candy, let him borrow things, and never told on him when he caused trouble and teased.

And he never told Mom.

· · • · ·

NOT LONG AFTERWARD, GREG and I put on our pajamas, grabbed blankets off our beds, and huddled on the couch, ready to be transported to another world. *Mary Poppins* was on TV.

Filled with energy from our immersion in the upbeat songs and the happy ending where the Banks family flies kites together in the park, Greg looked at me with his dimply grin. "Tomorrow morning, let's make us some kites and go fly them!"

"Yeah! Through the atmosphere!" I was all in.

"To the clearest air!" he sang.

The next morning, we hopped on our bikes to go buy materials. Greg rode fast, popping wheelies, plastic streamers whipping in the air. I rode my banana-seat bike, meandering, and occasionally tried to go no-handed for the feeling of balance and freedom.

Back at home with our supplies spread out over the living room floor—paper and glue from around the house, sticks from the yard, and string from the store—construction began. Greg had picked out appropriate sticks to use for the project. His were all similar in size and diameter. I looked down at my hodgepodge pile of twigs, none of which were long or good enough.

"I don't want to build a kite anymore! It's not going to fly anyway." I dropped my head.

"Here, take some of mine!" He handed me some sticks.

Greg's kite was solid and looked like it had flight potential. Mine was poorly constructed even with Greg's help. Each time I glued the paper to the sticks, my fingers would poke through the paper and rip it. I knew it would never take flight, but I didn't care anymore. I drew a pink-and-purple peace sign and the words *Can you dig it?* on my kite paper.

The children in *Mary Poppins* had won their father's attention, and we had benefited from their win. Their father, Mr. Banks, had changed from a gruff, distant parent into one who wanted to play with his kids. The possibilities—that people could change, that kids could be happy—were there, and I believed in something hopeful that day. I think Greg did too.

5

"JUST ONE"

DAD ATTENDED ALCOHOLICS ANONYMOUS meetings and received treatment for alcoholism at a local hospital as part of the deal he made with Mom to rejoin the family. AA recommended we have a dry house—no booze around to tempt him. Mom told us alcoholics can't have "just one."

The mood at home lifted like a bubble blown in the air, without direction and with the ever-present potential to pop. I'd catch Mom and Dad sharing a quick kiss in the kitchen in the morning and glimpses of what might have been romantic love. Whatever it was, it was new to me. I realized I had stopped licking my fingertips, just as unintentionally as I had started.

Kate, Greg, and I, in a rare collaboration, created a puppet show and performed it for our parents. We really wanted Mom and Dad to stop smoking. In the puppet show, there was a big race. The athlete puppet, expected to win the race, had taken up a bad habit: smoking. While he started the race strong, he coughed and hacked and fell to the ground just yards from the finish line. His lungs were too full of tar and nicotine to continue, and he lost. Soon after the show, our parents quit smoking, together.

Mom took up yoga and meditation, which she practiced at home with a book of poses. She seemed distracted and annoyed, even with all the extra breathing and stretching, yet we were a healthier family. The vibe at home felt different. Our new atmosphere was a cirrus cloud, tenuous and wispy. Within this tentative gaiety, I considered the possibility of a slumber party for my tenth birthday. Having friends overnight? It was now possible. Still, I knew one sip by Dad could cause his illness to barrel out of control down the tracks, wrecking our dry house.

Occasionally that year, 1976, Dad and I would go to the Knox College basketball games and cheer on the home team and a player named Dave "Woody" Woodward. Woody, who had small but wild, darting eyes and strong, hairy legs, broke many Knox College basketball records.

In the crowd we sat, Dad's polyester against my corduroy. The air smelled of wood and sweat. My heart thumped to the rhythm of the ball bouncing on the floor and raced with the players' jukes, passes, and jabs. Dad's black hair, treated with Grecian Formula and pomade, stayed where he combed it. To my nine-year-old self in my Dorothy Hamill haircut, this all felt gloriously normal.

During one competitive game, Woody halted his gait and held one arm out in the air, with his fingers spread and his other hand at his eye. The referee blew his whistle. The players were still. We watched intently as five guys got on their hands and knees and searched for Woody's lost contact. When it was found, Woody held it high in the air, and the crowd roared as if he had shot the winning basket.

There wasn't a three-point line, but there were shots from downtown, alley-oops, and all-nets. There were players who were hot and ran with that heat until they missed a few. We cheered hard, Dad and I, chanting, "We're number one" with the home team fans. Dad smiled so much it made me smile. We were winning, for the moment. Dad got up and said he had to use the bathroom, that he'd be back.

At halftime, I left our seats in the gymnasium and went in search of Dad and popcorn. As I navigated the hallway with the buzzing crowd, I stopped. Dad sat on the bench that lined the wall of the photographs of Knox athletes, laughing with a colleague and smoking a cigarette. I deflated and frowned as I stood next to him. He didn't explain or acknowledge my disappointment. All the buoyancy of the night, of the past few months, disappeared.

A week later, at the only party I remember my parents hosting, Dad laughed with a glass of liquor in hand, clinking the ice cubes against the sides, and I knew to expect a forthcoming derailment.

But the crash I was expecting didn't come from Dad, nor was it a loud, showy spectacle. It crept in slowly, through random comments Mom would spout, such as, "Be careful what you say on the phone. You don't know who is listening in." I'd ask who might be listening and why they would care what a kid like me said on the phone, and she'd get angry. Greg mentioned that since Dad took so many trips to the Soviet Union for the college, the government might be listening in on our calls. That made sense to me.

"Did you have a nice day at school, dear?" Mom would ask this question every day, but she'd be looking elsewhere, distracted. Looking back now, it's as if she was only pretending to play a mom. But at the time, her façade and her bizarre pronouncements were all I knew.

I didn't know what she was enduring; no one did. If she knew, she never suggested that she did or that she needed help.

Sometimes it seemed she was testing me, like the time she sat me down at the dining room table to tell me something important.

"Sit down for a minute. This is fascinating."

I leaned in, eager but wary.

As she started her story, she slowed down her speech and became dramatic, as if she had just taken the stage for a rehearsed monologue. "On my drive through Iowa—you remember I was there?—it was a lovely trip, and along the way, I noticed many things. The wildflowers were blooming along the roadside, and there were many signs to take in along the way. Signs of what? Well, one was a billboard that included a name of a town—Spillville. Now, isn't that just a hoot? Spillville!"

I nodded. It was kind of a funny name for a town.

"Well"—she was talking softer now and even more slowly—"there is a doctor here in Illinois named Spiller. This must explain why that girlfriend of Greg's has been recording all my conversations. You know she's been doing that, right?"

Her face went dark, and her eyes waited for my reaction. I shook my head.

"Well, it's clear to me it isn't just coincidence!" Her face was contorted, her eyes blazing.

"I don't understand, Mom. I'm trying."

"It isn't that difficult!"

I shut down, exited my body. It was like only a quarter of my brain rallied to stay present, to make it look like I was still there, while the rest drifted, hovered nearby.

She had tried her best to illuminate the obvious and ominous connections she saw between a billboard in Iowa, a doctor in Illinois, and why Greg's girlfriend was secretly recording her conversations, but I didn't get it, and that made her mad. I didn't understand like she wanted me to, and I wanted to leave.

I often upset her by trying to parse her words with rational thinking, something that was becoming important to me. "Mom, it just doesn't make sense. I can't follow your thinking. How exactly do those things relate to one another?" Even though her anger unnerved me, I was growing bolder and questioning her more. I wanted to help her make sense, not feel the pain of things that weren't true, and I wanted to show that I was not her. Normal teenage development in an abnormal situation.

Eventually, she lost (or quit; it was never clear) her job teaching French at the neighboring town's high school. She followed that up with a brief job at the Galesburg Landmark Café, where they offered French fare.

She quit within weeks after management refused her advice to have the menu changed from English to French and the waitstaff offer the specials in French to the Galesburg community diners. She never worked again, even though we sure seemed to need the money, given the way she refused to spend it and often regretted doing so when she did.

Every year, we were each allowed one new pair of shoes. One year, when Kate was a young teenager, Mom took her shopping in downtown Galesburg, and they came home with a pair of fake leather shoes. Kate winced as she tried them on for Dad. Mom told us they were a good price, if a bit too small. They would be just fine for Kate, she declared.

Dad inspected them. Having gone without shoes as a child prisoner and again later at the refugee camp, he believed footwear was important. He had once picked through a pile of donated shoes at the refugee camp to try to find two shoes that matched *and* fit. The shoes ended up being women's shoes, and he ruined them while playing soccer. Afterward, Nana made him kneel on sharp rocks as punishment. Yes, shoes were a hot button for Dad, and he was furious with Mom.

"No child of mine is going to wear shoes that are too small for them!" Dad marched Kate back to the shoe store, and Kate later said he told her to not look at the prices but to find a pair that fit well.

I'd looked on Mom's desk once to determine what she'd been spending her days doing and found a stack, several inches high, of carbon copy letters next to her typewriter. These were letters of complaint to various health care, financial, and retail corporations, admonishing them, accusing them of wrongdoing, claiming they owed her money, that they had sold her a bad product, that they'd intentionally taken her funds without her knowledge, charged her for services she didn't need, promised but didn't deliver, and so on. There were typos and strike-throughs throughout, and overall, her attempts to look professional instead unveiled her disorganized thoughts and paranoia.

· · • · ·

TO COPE WITH MOM being home all the time, I spent my days at friends' houses. In the summers starting when I was eleven, I'd hop on my bike at 9:00 a.m. and come home for the 6:00 p.m. dinner we had, every day, as a family. No one knew where I was all day long. No one asked.

Kate left for college at Knox, which was just a mile or two down the street. She lived on campus and rarely came home.

Except for dinner, Dad was out almost every night. Once again, he was a stranger to me. He'd had that first drink at the point in time when things seemed to get better for everyone, and he was still drinking. He drank all night, every night at the Elks Club. He'd arrive home sometime between midnight and one in the morning.

At night, I'd hold the sheets up to my chin and listen to train wheels screech in the distance before hearing the sharp cracks of breaking furniture and the deep wailing of a wounded animal—my dad. I'd wait, breathing but not breathing, until he'd fixed his midnight snack, rumbled and stumbled around, and then gone to sleep either on the couch downstairs or on a cot in the basement.

Dad's drinking intensified throughout my teenage years. Our family's focus, if you can say we had one, was his drinking, never Mom's brain health. Alcoholism was tangible—he drank too much liquor, and then he behaved recklessly. There was a clear cause and effect. Mom's brain illness was amorphous, and the social taboo of it eclipsed alcoholism. The clues were apparent and the case was closed: it was the alcoholic with the vodka in the living room.

6

CALVINS

WHEN I WAS THIRTEEN, my best friend, Sherry, wore her Calvin Klein jeans skintight. Her brown eyes, framed by full Brooke Shields eyebrows and long lashes, danced with deviousness. I envied her thick hair, thin waist, and woman's curves. My eyelashes were too short for the eyelash curler. Home perms had frizzed my thin, blond hair. My average frame supported my average weight, and Mom bought my Pizzazz-label jeans at Kmart.

Sherry and I planned one Friday night to walk from her house to the popular hangout of McDonald's on Henderson Street. We'd already stolen a can of beer from her mom to share along the way. As usual, our night started with an hour-long "getting ready" ritual. After makeup, we dressed. Sherry had already put her jeans in the dryer to shrink them, so they'd hug her curves. She stepped into them, tugged, pulled, wiggled her hips back and forth, and tugged and pulled again. Then she sat on her bed and leaned back, pulling and wiggling some more until they were up over her butt. At last, she sucked in her breath, her hip bones protruding, and zipped and buttoned. Afterward, in front of the mirror, she faced me and wrenched her neck to view her round rear. "How do they look?"

"They look great!" I sat on her bed, watched her longingly. The value of brand-name clothes was lost on my parents. Helping their children fit in through donning a label? Please. Mom preferred a classic look, one that didn't go out of style. "The fashion industry steals our money by changing trends overnight. The advertisers want to make you feel like you don't fit in unless you wear what they are selling. Good gracious. Don't fall for that!" I remember this as Mom's statement, but the sentiment could just as easily have come from Dad or Kate.

Finances also drove my parents' disdain for trends. Dad's salary was small despite being a tenured professor, and Mom wasn't working outside of the home. Both of my parents were naturally frugal, often to the extreme. Dad had grown up in poverty and war, which explained his thinking, but it was different for Mom. Her fixation on money sprang from secrecy (we didn't know how much of it she had), independence (she didn't share the money or knowledge of it with Dad), and paranoia (she thought everyone was after her things and her money).

One day as a thirteen-year-old, I summoned the nerve to say, "Mom, I need some new jeans."

"You have plenty of nice pants to wear." She said this with half her breath and half her attention as she was reaching into the cupboard and pulling out dishes.

"But I want jeans like the ones my friends wear."

"Followers follow trends. Creative people with ideas of their own do not." It was one of her mantras; I knew it by heart and should have expected it. While she focused on appearances, she also wore clothes she'd had for decades. She didn't spend money on clothes. Dad wrote her a check every month, and this is what she used to manage the household expenses.

I guessed she was right, and a big part of me agreed: I wanted to be creative. But I had asked people to start calling me Liz instead of Liza because I thought it would help me fit in, and I also wanted to wear clothes that didn't make me stand out, clothes that allowed me to blend in, neither following nor leading.

· · • · ·

KIDS IN JUNIOR HIGH talked about how much money they'd earned working on farms in the summer. With Calvin Klein jeans on my mind, I applied at the employment office by the high school for a job detasseling corn at Pioneer Farms. If they decided to hire me, they'd call me during the summer, and I'd start work the following week. The job paid minimum wage to kids still too young to legally work in other trades.

Detasseling corn—taking the tassel off the top of the stalk and dropping it on the ground so the plant can't pollinate itself—allows for pollination by a different variety of corn plant growing in the next row.

I got the call early in July to start the following Monday. At 6:00 a.m., a dozen or more kids my age and older boarded a Pioneer Farms bus with lunch bags, sleepy eyes, and little instruction. I'd dressed in long pants and long sleeves, as recommended, for what was going to be a ninety-degree day. We'd get to our destination somewhere in rural Illinois by 6:30 or 7:00 a.m. to begin work. The apprehension of the unknown, the disorientation of getting up when it was still dark, and the breakfast I'd forced down because I knew it would be a long day all gave me a butterflies-in-the-stomach feeling.

Though I was still shy and lacking confidence, something told me I could do it and it was going to be worth it. The Calvin Kleins called. I imagined wearing the jeans and the way they'd fit snugly but comfortably. I wouldn't look the way Brooke Shields or even Sherry did in their Calvins, but I'd be closer to that ideal.

The crew leaders, girls and boys just a couple of years older than I was, hollered out the basics: "Don't miss a tassel, and work fast!" No one wanted to be the last one to finish a row and come out of the field to find the rest of the crew watching and waiting.

Tucked inside the vast fields, I trudged through rows of corn, ankle-deep in mud, and inhaled the grassy smells of tilled black earth, fresh crops, and manure. The job of removing tassels required me to look up to the top of the plant as I walked through the green tunnel while mature leaves flapped against my body. At one point as I looked up, trying to keep pace with the others, the sharp edge of a dew-covered leaf ripped through my cornea. I screamed and rubbed my eye. Scared I'd fall behind, I continued my stride. I skipped several stalks and rubbed my swollen eye, as it had started to pulse and itch. I labored the rest of the day peering through squinting eyes, seeing nothing but blurry stalks, tassels, husks, and leaves. I reached high above my head to remove tassels while angry, rough razor leaves sliced my face and neck.

I think all thirteen-year-olds should detassel corn in Illinois for three weeks in ninety-degree heat and humidity. It was the hardest job I ever had. My dad beamed as I slogged into the house after that first day in the fields, mud caked up to my waist, my lower arms and face burned from the sun and torn up by leaves.

Mom scrunched up her face. "I don't see why you couldn't find a job in an air-conditioned office." I opened my mouth to respond, to say there were no office jobs for thirteen-year-olds, but she left the room before I could answer. That happened a lot.

The character-building experience of my summer job also provided my personal path to addiction. The older, therefore cooler, girls would take breaks at the end of each row in the long cornfields and light up. At first, I'd sit a good distance away with the quiet nonsmokers and chomp on an apple, shoulders hunched, exhausted and overheated from the work. I watched as the cool smokers laughed and sang, gazed as they dragged hard on their cigarettes and then got up and danced.

One of the girls, with a gymnast's physique and a voice that sounded rough and joyful at the same time, sang a popular song by Juice Newton,

"Queen of Hearts," but interjected her boyfriend's name, Peter Tart. I thought about all the things she probably did with and for Peter Tart, knowing it wasn't really smart, and I felt giddy and dirty. I couldn't decide—was I envious or disgusted?

I wanted in, knowing I didn't belong. I made up reasons I didn't fit with these girls. I told myself it was because my dad was an immigrant from Russia or because I came from an academic family. But deep down, I was certain a frumpy, shy girl like me would never mesh with these strong, self-assured girls from other backgrounds.

Smoking was ancillary to the tight-knit group I was sure they must be, to the gregariousness and the joy that seemed to fill them up and burst out of them in laughter and song. But smoking was part of the package and the only part that was accessible to me.

As luck would have it, Sherry's mom, Marty, smoked menthol cigarettes. Sherry and I started smoking by standing in her first-floor bathroom, just off the kitchen, taking long puffs of Marty's cigarettes and holding them in as long as we could. Our aim was to feel dizzy. And it worked. So we did it again. And again. Then we bought our own cigarettes. We began to feel we "needed" a cigarette more often than we did. We were closer to cool, and that closeness included warmth and fire. I needed the warmth, and Sherry liked to play with fire.

Marty had black, shiny hair with loose curls and big brown eyes. Like Sherry, she wore a lot of makeup and liked to have fun, even though she was a mom, a fact I wouldn't have believed if I hadn't seen it for myself.

Marty called me *Lizzie*. I liked the way she said *Lizzie* with her cherry-red lips framing her super-white, slightly crooked teeth into a vertical, glossy smile. Marty made me realize that not all moms warned of bugged phones; some moms liked to laugh with their kids. Moms didn't all drive ten miles per hour down the street and scowl the entire time they shopped with their kids for clothes, then come home with nothing. Marty would speak to Sherry of her day, laugh with her about silly things, trust her with jobs around the house, and get mad when Sherry didn't do them.

Galesburg was a small town, and Marty, like my dad, drank at night at the Elks Club. He was so proud to have found a place to belong, to have joined the Elks, that he wrote a letter to Mom's aunt Hilda and uncle Ivan about it, eager to gain their respect.

"I saw your dad again last night at the Elks Club!" Marty said to me one day, smiling.

I wilted. She must have seen Dad drunk. Did she wonder why Mom was never there? Mom never went with Dad to the Elks Club. I couldn't see Mom at what I imagined a local bar scene looked like, and I supposed she didn't want any part of it.

"He has the most amazing stories from his childhood!" Marty went on. "He is such a remarkable man, and he's so smart!"

I started to feel icky. I imagined Dad and Marty laughing together, sitting next to each other on barstools with a standing crowd of people who'd grown up in Galesburg, who worked in the factories and farms, who owned small businesses or worked at them, listening to my foreign-born father tell the tragic tales of his youth in Eastern Europe filled with details he never shared with us. I didn't like that he was fun with other people and such a grump with us. It made me feel like he was two people, and I didn't like either of them anymore.

Marty didn't mention Dad much after that time, which was fine with me. He had already begun descending from the pedestal I had placed him on in my younger years.

7

DOT IN THE DISTANCE

"YOU'RE TOO CLOSE!" FROM a metal-framed lawn chair, Mom jab-pointed her finger past Dad and his camera, the driveway, and the basketball hoop, indicating the neighbor's bushes. "Move over there." A few sticky strands of hair clung to her tight jaw.

We were there too, the three of us kids standing oldest to youngest by the back door, against the rough stucco exterior, not interfering. The jagged stucco poked my back, and I pushed against it. It helped to feel the poke instead of the rock in my stomach.

I stayed quiet. One wrong word from anyone and Dad might lose it and flee. When sober, in the face of conflict, he was a hare in a storm—gone. Fast.

My insides rattled as a freight train's horn boomed. For seven years, I'd lived near the tracks, and I still felt fear from the sound and its aftermath. A discordant metal-on-metal screech. I'd learned that if the train operator sees something on the tracks, they won't be able to stop the train, that it takes about a mile—even in an emergency—to come to a full stop. The barreling beast of commotion was unstoppable. My body's freeze-or-flight response, which also happened when Dad was drunk or Mom was irrational, was automatic.

Mom swung her head to shake her hair into better placement for the photo.

Dad grinned. He rarely smiled full on. The sound of the train faded into the cornfields, and he took a step backward, seeming to beam with hope that he'd soon freeze time with his photo. "How's this?"

He was happy. My spirit lifted for a moment, but I knew better than to expect his joy to last.

It was her birthday, or maybe Mother's Day, but not their anniversary. They had stopped celebrating their anniversary a few years before. It made sense: Why celebrate something that makes you miserable?

"Keep going." Mom flung her head back and sat spine-straight on the edge of the folding chair, knees together and to the side, shoulders back, chin up, head tilted. She forced a smile. The rock in my stomach knocked around as she posed and bossed Dad around.

Dad crouched and moved back a few more steps. His hands still cradled the camera, masking his face. The black, sharp-angled Kodak had a silver section on top, which, along with his shiny, wide forehead, caught the sun every now and then. He pressed his eye to the viewfinder, and a couple of wild Russian eyebrow hairs rested on the rim of his glasses. Sweat started beading at his recessed hairline. "How about now?"

Her eyes narrowed as she gestured toward the trees across our small-town lawn. "No! Too close! Move there, by that tree." She pressed her white cotton blouse with the palm of her hands so it lay flat on her stomach, her tiny waist. Her beauty: her.

Dad's grin was gone, his shoulders hunched. "Cathy, you'll appear as a dot in the distance!" he yell-mumbled. If nothing else, around us, he was a mumbler. I figured it was safer that way; we never knew what would set her off.

I knew the moment he wanted to capture had long passed. There was no alcohol in the house, but if Mom said the wrong word—the word guaranteed to make him flee—he could leave now and be standing at the Elks Club bar in ten minutes.

That word during those years, the one that riled him whenever she used it in front of us, was his given name, Vasily.

· · • · ·

MOM HAD WIELDED HER Vasily weapon once at Dad's favorite fishing spot, Green Oaks. I'd already enjoyed fishing at Green Oaks with Dad on several occasions, and when he was in a good mood, he'd hook my worms and call me his butterball; when he wasn't, he'd yell about me not being a real fisherman if I couldn't hook my own worms. On this day, we experienced forced family time: a torturous picnic with muggy, blistering heat, a stagnant lake, and mosquitoes. We were the only ones crazy enough to think it was a good day for a picnic. We sat in the sun at an old, splintered wood picnic table, kids on one side, parents on the other.

I wanted this adventure to work; I liked the idea of our family being on a normal family outing. My friends' families took weekend days and picnicked, played games, laughed, and talked. Why couldn't we?

I decided to do my part and not fight with Greg—that is, until he reached into his jean shorts and pulled out his Swiss Army knife. He met my gaze and smirked as he started carving into the bench between us. I kicked his foot. I had poked the beast. He stared me dead in the eyes as he stuck his index finger high up his nostril, brought out a glob of snot, and stuck it on my arm.

Payback was always a thousand times worse. I backed off.

The tall native grass and plants of the Green Oaks prairie had grown since the last supervised burn. Pollen added haze to the already thick air above the field. We ate the sandwiches Mom brought, batting at the flies and mosquitoes. The heat, the bugs, the pretending left everyone crabby, wanting to escape. Only hope must have kept us there, the hope of being a normal family.

We alternated taking bites of our sandwiches and wiping away sweat. Mom looked toward the lake and smiled. "The fishing might be good today, kids, with this heat, or do I have that turned around? *Vasily* should know. Vasily?"

Dad glared at Mom. "How many times? How many times? Damn it!" he huffed. "Why can't you say 'your dad' or 'your father'? I'm their dad, damn it all!" Then he was gone, marching off into the prairie. His long-sleeved shirt and black polyester pants, protecting his allergic skin from the sun, clung to his wide waist and skinny bowlegs. His beige fishing hat, darker around the rim from dirt and sweat, shielded his face. No one said anything as we watched him walk down the path, toward the road, until we could no longer see him.

We waited. The sun set, and the mosquitoes swarmed. After several hours, we packed it up to drive the seventeen miles to our house without Dad.

I still don't get it. Maybe it was *how* she said his name. Was it too intimate? Or disrespectful? We called him *Dad*, of course. When I was younger, I'd call him *Père*, French for "Dad," and he'd call me *apple*. And we'd giggle. Did hearing *Vasily* from her make him feel more Russian than he wanted to feel? Did he want to be more American? The guys at the Elks Club called him *Bill*. He didn't like his name mispronounced. He'd rather those people who couldn't get it right just call him *Bill*. He didn't hide from his Russian identity. Our house was full of Russian wooden figures, chess sets, and photographs of onion-bulb-steepled cathedrals. He was a Russian professor of modern languages. Was he a Russian in America? A Russian American?

On the way home, I stared out the window into the darkness, the woods, the cornfields, and the small towns we passed, hoping to catch sight of him, hoping he'd get in the car and we'd all go home together.

I FIXED MY ATTENTION on Dad's growing frustration as he tried to take Mom's photo in the backyard. As I wondered if he was going to leave in a huff like he had at Green Oaks, I pushed my back into the stucco to see how hard I had to press before a sharp edge pierced my skin. Dad fiddled with the camera, and Mom primped and posed.

Greg rolled his eyes before saying, "How long does it take to take a friggin' picture? This must be a world record."

I admired and hated that he could impact a tense situation any way he saw fit. Greg could divert the train, while I was stuck watching the collision, helpless.

Kate elbowed Greg in the ribs.

"Ouch! Cut it out. How much you wanna bet Dad bolts?" Greg's contraband Marlboros were in his front shirt pocket, hidden behind his tan jacket.

I wanted one.

"He's gonna split. I can feel it." Greg hoped Dad would bolt so he could escape as well. Cigarettes, girls, and his new taste for beer were calling.

Dad finally moved to where Mom told him to, and he snapped the *damn picture, for god's sake.*

Dad didn't flee, not physically. But the almost-warm moment between my parents had vanished, replaced by the usual iceberg of unspoken misunderstandings. After Dad snapped the *damn picture*, he went inside before the rest of us, to the comfort of his Archie Bunker armchair, where he turned the Cubs game on and lulled himself into a trance by rubbing his mustache between his thumb and forefinger. He was good at leaving, but he was also good at staying and tuning us out.

Mom, in the kitchen, worked to nourish us with an undercooked rice-and-tuna casserole and canned fruit smothered in Jell-O. My stomach hurt, and our dinner that evening, not unlike others, was quick and quiet. Except for the crunchy casserole.

· · • · ·

MOM NEVER WANTED A close-up. Even after the zoom mechanism was available on all cameras, she'd make Dad move back, back, back until she was content that . . . what? Her wrinkles wouldn't show? Then, of course, he'd zoom her in for a close-up, never letting on that she wasn't still a dot in the distance. The soft curves of her cheekbones, her dark, plucked eyebrows, her grace would all be translated onto photo paper.

I thought at the time Mom was too worried about her looks and that's why she was weird about Dad taking her picture. But it could have been her yet-to-be-diagnosed illness. Her brain read strange and scary meanings into the things going on around her. She believed people could hear her thoughts. She perceived danger and "strange coincidences" from connections she made but no one else could understand. She feared technology and probably saw the camera as dangerous. I'd heard that in some cultures people thought photography could steal your soul. Maybe Mom thought so too.

After Dad had his film developed from that day in the backyard, I studied the picture of Mom. The dot in the distance was hard to make out. Her vast smile and graceful stature were a blur.

· · • · ·

THE PHOTOGRAPHS GAVE DAD something firm and lasting, easy to hold and share, and a voice. Perhaps photos made sense when his wife did not. She remained his greatest love and his greatest misery. For me, my parents are both dots in the distance, and I'm searching for the zoom.

8

THE HOUSE THAT FIT THE RUG

"CATHY," DAD IMPLORED, "THIS house is more than we can afford. Interest rates are through the roof." Mom had inherited an Oriental rug that was too big for the rooms in our one-and-a-half-story bungalow by the tracks. We moved into a new house on Broad Street, in an area sometimes referred to as "Professor Row." The train's horn blared in the distance there, a little easier to ignore, but still a reminder of my early-childhood fears, a reminder of all things unstoppable. As the new owner of my sister's baby-blue Schwinn ten-speed, I began finding more ways to leave my parents.

It was a sunny day when Mom marched into the house with a stray, white fluff ball of a dog. She'd rescued him from the playground where she'd noticed he'd been searching for scraps and attention for several days. The dog, a spitz, dropped his pointy muzzle to our hardwood floors and darted around like a rodent, sniffing, not paying attention to Tawny, who was old and lay curled up on the couch, uninterested.

The dog's true owners eventually came forward, their appearance causing the fluff ball to lower his triangle ears and cower. I knelt and petted the dog while Mom convinced the owners to let us keep him. Mom named him Chou Chou. *Mon petit chou* is a French term of endearment used for children, meaning "my little cabbage."

After the owners left—without a care in the world, it seemed—Chou Chou walked over to a side table and lifted his little leg. Pungent-smelling urine splattered the table and rug. From deep in her throat, Mom screamed, "*Noooooooo!*" She scooped up Chou Chou and took him outside. Yelling, "No!" and moving him outside each time she caught him peeing didn't do the trick. To make matters worse for himself, Chou Chou only relieved himself on the Oriental rug: the rug that had put my parents deep in debt and in a state of financial insecurity.

Mom deported our adopted dog—the dog that barked a strained but adorable *arf*, the dog we were chin-in-the-air proud of and certain we'd saved from abuse—to the outermost part of the backyard. Banished, chained to a post, and given a doggie house with *Chez Chou* painted on it as conciliation, he lived in exile for his crime of not being housebroken.

The house that fit the rug—a poorly insulated 1920s Georgian colonial-style edifice on Broad Street—admittedly had curb appeal. It had a gray stucco exterior, and two white Greek columns rose on either side of the red front door. Everything on the outside appeared stable and symmetrical.

During the time when we lived in the house that fit the rug, Mom's unhinging and Dad's drinking both intensified and crashed into my teenage rebellion. After Kate left for college, the tension at home seemed to get even worse. She hadn't been spending much time at home before moving; when she wasn't working, she was at her boyfriend's house. Yet her complete absence loosened the ligaments that held our family in place. Perhaps with his firstborn favorite no longer watching, Dad finally felt free to accelerate his descent.

I eased into the role of juvenile delinquent by breaking the law and school rules daily. I continued to get good grades in junior high and played in the band, and teachers trusted me. But temptations were everywhere, activities that could fill the void and satisfy my sense of teenage curiosity. I found warmth in the fire that lit the cigarettes and joints I'd started to smoke; in the sun and in heavy metal music; in the hot breath of a boy hard against me; in the rapid heartbeat I'd feel when stealing from stores.

One weekend night, Sherry and I asked two boys, one quite older, if they'd score us a bottle of Jack Daniel's. Sherry knew what to ask for. We met them in the McDonald's parking lot, where they delivered the bottle, and we purchased our chasers before walking back to Sherry's.

The winter wind whistled through the cracks of the doors and windows at Sherry's mom's old home. Her brother and sister were at their dad's for the night, and her mom was at the Elks Club. Pam, our friend from school, was dropped off at Sherry's by her mom.

Pam's mom let her have most anything she wanted. When Pam screamed at her mom or made demands, her mom would say, "Oh, Pam!" and cackle before giving in. I'd learned to smoke stick cigarettes in Pam's backyard at nightly summer bonfires after seventh grade. We'd pick up a dried five- or six-inch stick from the ground, put one end in the fire till it blazed yellow and red, then inhale the smoke of burned maple or oak.

The three of us plunked down on Sherry's living room couch and passed the bottle of Jack back and forth, pinching our noses and quickly slurping down gulps of Coke through straws after each swig of whiskey.

Sherry and I had figured a fifth would be enough. We didn't know. Up to that point, we'd only split a beer here and there, stolen from her mom's refrigerator. Before we realized we'd drunk far too much, we'd finished the bottle and were stumbling around the house. Our laughter was strong, our inhibitions weak. We decided our blue jeans were too tight, so we took them off. Then the boys who'd bought us the booze stopped by.

I remember riding Sherry's brother's little bike, knees to chest in my cotton underwear and sweater, down the snow-covered stairs of her back porch. "Wheeeeeee!" *Thump. Thump. Thump. Thump.*

I remember wiping out at the bottom of the stairs and not feeling any pain or even the cold snow on my bare legs.

I remember laughing more than I'd laughed in my life.

I remember being on all fours in the driveway, howling at the moon in unison with Sherry's Siberian husky, Tasha.

I remember laughing until tears poured down my face and I no longer knew if I was happy or sad.

I remember lying down in the snow and looking at the stars.

I remember the sky spinning and my stomach turning.

I remember running to the upstairs bathroom and vomiting and heaving and vomiting and heaving. Again. And again. And when I was empty, I made my way slowly down the stairs toward the living room.

I remember seeing one of my friends lying across the couch with her head on the lap of one of the boys. Her eyes were closed, and his hand was underneath her underwear, cradling her crotch.

I remember not knowing if she was happy or asleep.

I remember I was uncomfortable, and I met his eyes from the stairs.

I remember not looking away, not letting him off the hook, just in case.

I remember he got up, and he and his friend left.

I don't remember anything else.

Sherry and I later laughed about that night and referred to "our friend Jack" as an inside joke. Absent attentive parents, we were lost, but free. We were trying to define a space for ourselves. We wanted to feel. Anything. We risked so much of our innocence, our childhood, to feel. Anything. Or was it to feel nothing?

· · • · ·

THE FOLLOWING SUMMER, ON a warm night with crickets chirping, Sherry and I pitched a tent in her backyard. Sherry had managed to sneak a tiny bottle of peppermint schnapps out of her house. Ever since "our friend Jack," we'd had a hard time getting liquor down. So at about 10:00 p.m., we walked the quiet, dark streets to the nearby 7-Eleven for snacks and a chaser.

Alone in the store, except for the woman working the register, we browsed the fluorescent-lit aisles. Without thinking, I grabbed a fifteen-cent long stick Jolly Rancher and slid it into my back pocket. Watermelon. My favorite.

I flinched as my arm was yanked at the elbow by the thick, middle-aged woman who was working the night shift. She pulled me to the counter, held me there with her tight grip, as if I would run, which I wouldn't and couldn't, because my body wouldn't move. With her other hand, she clutched the receiver of the store phone and used her index finger to dial. She puffed out her chest and stared me down. "Officer Dan just left. Shouldn't take him long to get back here."

Sherry's eyebrows were up, lips tight, yet her brown eyes were dancing with delight. This made me smile, but I was in over my head. Recently, I'd been hanging out at the mall with girls who stole like trained thieves. They stole from Claire's Boutique while the women employees in heavy makeup and big hair stood in the back and gossiped. I'd pinched a cheap necklace the second time I was with those girls and felt the rush. I felt like trash every time I wore the fake gold around my neck, and that seemed deserved.

Sherry and I sat in the slippery, black back seat of the shiny police car and giggled. We often giggled when we shouldn't: in band, class lectures, and youth group at her church.

At the Galesburg police station, I was booked, fingerprinted, humiliated. Mom picked us up, and I wondered what she thought about what I had done, though she didn't say a word. She dropped Sherry off and brought me home. She said, "We'll wait up until your father gets home."

Later, I sat hunched on the wood stairs while Dad stood in the foyer, facing me, feet wide, swaying. "What have we taught you about stealing?" He delivered a short lecture that I didn't listen to because he was drunk and I was frozen. What mattered was how mad he'd get. I waited for escalating anger that never came. He passed out afterward on the couch in the den.

I was hiding out in my bedroom the next day when Kate came in and immediately asked, "Why did you do it?" She seemed to think I'd have an answer. I suppose if she ever decided to steal, she would know why she did it, but I couldn't verbalize the connection between my actions and what I was feeling or thinking.

"I don't know," I answered. "I just wanted to see if I could get away with it, I guess." My stomach hurt as if all my words, all the letters, were tangled and disintegrating in gastric juice.

She shook her head. "I don't understand." Her disappointment was worse than Dad's. She had never done anything wrong in her life, as far as I knew. Her face had never experienced foundation, blush, or mascara. She didn't drink, smoke, or steal. She never had that kind of urge. Or if she did, she never succumbed to it. I couldn't explain why I had.

She wasn't a sister who'd comfort me, joke about what happened, or tell me that stealing a piece of candy was no big deal, that lots of times kids do things on impulse and that it didn't make me a bad person. That I shouldn't be too hard on myself. No, I'd let her down. Kate, the only family member who seemed to have it together, who did well in school, played on the tennis team, had a boyfriend, and found legitimate reasons to leave the house. A blanket of shame covered me and left me cold and nauseous.

· · ● · ·

TO EASE THE ENERGY crisis, President Carter had urged US citizens to keep their thermostats at sixty-five degrees. Over the years, Dad did more than follow President Carter's suggestion. If sixty-five degrees could save energy, what could fifty-five degrees do to help his heating bill in the poorly insulated house that they couldn't afford but that fit the Oriental rug? I curled up under my covers at night, relying on my own hot air for warmth. I created an open space around my face under the blankets so I didn't suffocate, where my breath could gather and create heat to defrost my nose.

Mom walked around rubbing her hands together to generate friction; she told us to "just put on another sweater" and we'd be fine. Greg said he could see his breath. In my room, I'd blow air out and look down my nose to see if I could see anything. Sometimes I did.

Often after Dad left the house, Greg, wearing a muscle shirt and an air of defiance, marched up to the thermostat mounted on the wall next to the piano. In one swift, spiteful shift, he'd turn the dial to seventy degrees with a look of sublime satisfaction. Though Dad wasn't there, I could feel his disappointment. I didn't want anyone fighting. Greg's bold rebellion unnerved me.

"Who turned the heat up in this house?" Dad demanded when he came home. Silence. Greg would turn the dial back down after the house was warm, but Dad was nobody's fool. The thermostat was down, but tension was mounting.

The household was also cold in other ways. Mom and Dad didn't discuss the events of their days or the events of the world. They didn't go out to dinner or out with friends. They didn't host dinner parties or attend them. They each went about their days doing their own things, following their own routines.

Mom spent much of her time in the kitchen, moving items from here to there and back to here, taking the phone off the hook or sometimes off the wall, closing the blinds, writing and posting notes, and whispering to beings we couldn't see. One day, when I went downstairs to the laundry room to look for a pair of jeans, I heard a noise on the other side of the basement. When I walked over to investigate, I found Mom with an eye patch over one eye, jogging on the balls of her feet around the perimeter of the small cement-floored room.

"What are you doing?" I asked.

She kept jogging in her dainty fashion. "Jogging," she said without expression.

I didn't ask about the eye patch.

· · • · ·

MOM STILL PREPARED DINNER and cleaned up after meals, but sometimes she just sat in the living room with a book on her lap, doing nothing. She did everything she could to keep the happenings on the inside of our house from the outside world. Or just as likely, she was keeping something she perceived outside of our house from getting in. She kept our shades and blinds closed day and night. Natural light, sneaking through the closed horizontal blinds in our living room, lined Mom's Oriental rug. Thin lines of light, broken up by a few inches of darkness, gave her rug a prison-bar overlay.

Mom and Dad shared no loving glances, no understanding gestures now. There were no more morning kisses, just sour faces. Dad mumbled so much I wondered how Mom knew what he was saying, but she must have, because she always had a response, a retort that conveyed, "Oh yeah? Well, same to you!" They projected their chill onto us, their kids, whom they'd notice every now and then with mild surprise.

Our only family time consisted of suffering through mandatory and painful 6:00 p.m. dinners. The conversation was stiff and slim and the indigestion substantial. Mom had one meal we all liked—a chicken, soup, and rice casserole. She prepared it well until she didn't, or couldn't; after that, hard, uncooked rice stuck in our teeth. But we said nothing; we kept eating the casseroles hoping next time it would be better. Say and do nothing and hope for better—the theme of our lives.

ONE DAY, I RETURNED home from school eager as always to race to my room unseen. If I made it past the foyer to the stairs, I was in the clear. As my foot touched that first step, Mom said, "Liza, I need to tell you something."

I froze. Mom stood in the middle of the living room, beckoning me. Her messy, home-dyed hair framed her face as she motioned me over.

As I stood before her, she made sure I was listening by looking into my eyes. "Something very disturbing happened to me at the eye doctor," she said. "Do you know what he did?" She pointed at her pupil. "He shot a microchip into my eye! Poof!"

She didn't move her bulging, searching eyes from mine. I looked at my intelligent mom, squinted to search her eyes, knowing there was nothing there to find.

Mom shook her head. "How else could it have gotten in there?"

My mother trusted me enough in that moment to share something she was convinced about but that she also might have known I'd see as absurd. I was not equipped to handle it. I left her standing there, distressed and alone. My body, with its shoulders heavy, heart pounding, and breath short, joined my mind, which had snuck out to the backyard when Mom started talking about the microchip. My body and my brain hovered by our dog Chou Chou, who barked his rough little *arf*. He remained in the backyard, chained, alone.

• • • • •

THE MIDWESTERN SUMMER SUN softened the asphalt shingles on Sherry's roof. I knew this because she and I sunbathed on it, naked. We climbed out her sister's dormer bedroom window onto the angled rooftop and lay down our beach towels and Marlboro Reds. *Cowboy killers*, we called them.

Without a flat surface for our sun-brewed iced teas, we placed our tumblers on the windowsill, an arm's reach away. We knelt on our towels, feeling the freedom of our exposed breasts in the wind, and scanned the tree-lined block of two-story 1930s homes in Galesburg, Illinois, for any voyeurs before pretending no one could see us anyway.

We were interested in growing up fast, spending our days seeking thrills and heat. The warmth of the sun on every square inch of my bare body filled me, excited me, and most of all gave Sherry and me something to giggle about.

Sherry, lying there with her tiny waist and childbearing hips, her eyes closed, said, "I'm going to name my first child Ashley."

I'd never known an Ashley before. Only a character on a soap opera. The name seemed sensual to me, probably because of the soap character, and like a name Sherry would choose.

"I approve," I said. "I like the name."

Sherry's early maternal calling didn't surprise me, yet I had a hunch it was the sex she wanted as much as the child. Her olive skin glistened from sweat-infused baby oil. Her thick, auburn hair spread Medusa-like across her towel. Her eyes, unusually bare of makeup, looked at me, waiting for me to share.

I had no name chosen for a future child. I felt nothing but the warmth of the sun, the hottest rays congregating in my pelvis. I couldn't imagine a life growing in me. I'd recently learned that it's possible to get pregnant the first time you do it. I wasn't planning on doing it anytime soon.

Like many moms, mine often said, "You kids are driving me crazy!" I thought the toil of raising three kids must have something to do with the strange way Mom behaved. Children might make me like her.

Sherry's eyes were closed again. "What will you name your first child?" Her voice was soft and sleepy.

"Maybe I won't ever have kids," I said as I realized it. The whole idea of mothering was fraught with sadness and trouble. What was the upside? I couldn't fathom unconditional love.

"Really?"

I let out a stuck breath. "Really."

After a few minutes, Sherry sat up. "Oh, Liz, everyone has kids!"

I turned my head to face the horizon and wondered if she was right. Would I have kids? Would I become my mom?

9

WHITE NOISE

I STARED OUT THE window of my blue bedroom at our garage, where I'd hidden earlier to smoke a cigarette. Beyond my small midwestern town, the harvest-ready cornfields blazed against a red-and-purple sunset. A freight train roared in the distance as I caught Dad making tracks to the car.

My parents' fight had been the sober kind, where not much was said, where afterward the air suffocated, and Dad, Mom, my brother, and I each pursued our own paths to relief. Dad's path, as usual, was leading him to a bottle, so I set up white noise by my twin bed: a boom box tuned to early '80s Top 40 and a vacillating fan on high.

Greg would've been living on campus on the other side of town had he not been expelled for his low GPA and a run-in with the campus police the year before. He couldn't keep it together enough to maintain his freedom from Broad Street. He was once more living back in the house I was so desperate to depart.

At midnight, I woke to pounding footsteps, slamming doors, cracking furniture.

Dad shouted to Mom with slurred speech, "Damn it, Cathy! Get down here!"

Tentatively, I emerged to see Mom tying her robe sash, her cheekbones angular and eyes resigned. She stopped, looked toward the stairs, and waited outside the door for a moment. They had been married for twenty-two years. This mayhem was a time-honored routine. I couldn't understand why they stayed together when divorce was common. I'd asked Mom why they didn't divorce and said that if they were waiting for me to graduate high school, they didn't have to. She told me the same thing each time I brought it up: "It's complicated. Maybe when you're older, you'll understand."

At fifteen, I no longer felt like a child, but I also couldn't move or think when his quiet, professorial nature flipped to belligerent, or her lucidity to absurdity. I stood in the hallway and watched her as she walked down the stairs. I waited in the corner, eclipsed by the dark shadows. I tried not to let out my breath; my heart pounded in my ears. I felt the penetrating vibrations of Dad's booming voice. Mom's whisper.

They continued this way in the foyer at the bottom of the stairs, him confrontational and her hushing him, until the front door opened.

My brother Greg stood as tall as Dad at five ten but was lean and agile. He wore his Levi's and his collared shirt tight, his hair feathered and sprayed. Dad was thick now, mostly in the middle, where the sweater he wore day in and day out caught the droppings of his food. Greg's sandy blond hair and blue eyes contrasted with Dad's black hair and dark-hazel eyes.

Greg tripped into the foyer and struggled to regain his balance.

"Where in the hell have you been?" Dad said, turning his drunken attention from my mother to Greg.

"Out." Greg smirked, still wobbling. "What about you?"

Dad, not at all amused, yelled at Greg for drinking and being out late, missing the irony. As he bellowed, he moved toward Greg, who backed his way out of the house. They ended up in the front yard, where I could no longer see or hear what was happening.

Mom came upstairs seeming lucid, determined. "We are leaving. Get your things for the night."

We'd never left the house in the middle of the night. My legs felt weak, and my stomach dropped, yet I knew I'd follow her. At this moment, she was my most functional parent. I assumed we were going to a hotel, and that sounded okay. I would get to go back to sleep. And escape until the light and promise of a new day.

Greg and Dad were nowhere in sight as we pulled away from the house. Mom drove us around town for a half hour, going at her usual snail's crawl. In the distance, a train horn sounded. The streets were dark, and the old Chevette bounced over the brick roads. The warm autumn air smelled of smoldering bonfires and rotting leaves.

Why were we driving without an apparent destination? Maybe she was waiting for Dad and Greg to pass out. I hoped we'd eventually just go back to the house and sleep in our own beds. We didn't say much to each other; we never really did. With our heads full of thoughts and our mouths empty of words, we rode in silence.

Mom drove into the parking lot of the Motel 6, next door to the corner liquor store where I'd recently passed for twenty-one. The sign read: $19.99/night.

This is an acceptable choice, I thought. *Let's do this. Let's get some sleep.* I imagined going to school, pretending this fucked-up night hadn't happened.

Mom parked and told me to wait. At the front desk, she talked with the hotel employee. She spoke with her hands, her gestures familiar—contained yet crazy.

After a minute, she strutted out, scowling. She slid into the driver's seat and said, "Highway robbery!" flinging her head to the side and backing the car up.

It was a motel, for god's sake. What other options do we have?

Mom pulled up to a house canopied by mature oak and ash trees, the home of a colleague of Dad's who also happened to be the father of Kate's high school boyfriend. Kate had had a close relationship with this family while she dated the son, but other than that, our families didn't know each other well. Our family didn't know *any* family well. Yet here we were, at 1:30 a.m., standing on their doorstep. Better to wake up a family, air our dirty laundry, punish Dad, than pay for a hotel.

We were invited in without hesitation and ushered to a spare room containing stored items. We moved some boxes, piles of clothes, and blankets to find the beds. Sleep came fast in the stillness of a strange house.

Mom nudged me awake just after dawn, and we snuck out despite the welcoming aroma of biscuits and bacon in the air. I showered, rode to school with a friend, and attended classes and band practice just like any other day. I skipped lunch to avoid deepening the discomfort in my gut.

At home after school, I hoped to head straight to my bed. My brother, slouched at the kitchen table, stretched out his legs; his untied Nike high-tops blocked my path. I looked up and gasped at the red-and-blue shine beneath his eye, his purple fat lip. The sunset colors across his face blurred together, and my stomach turned.

"Seriously?" He laughed. "You think this is bad? You should see the other guy."

I collapsed into a chair next to him. His face, protective humor, and bravado—all evidence of what was wrong with our family, of what I'd hoped to drown out. As much as I wanted to, I couldn't look away.

10

BORDERLINE

MOM LEFT FOR SEATTLE the summer I was sixteen to visit Aunt Carol with no return date. I didn't think much about her trip at the time. There was no special occasion, and she didn't ask me to come, so I sucked in all the air in the house I could. Without the constant checking over my shoulder, the sneaking, the worry that she was just around the corner whispering to nobody, I relaxed.

My job at Just Pants, a clothing store at the mall where we sold more than just pants, required me to work many nights until 9:30 p.m. After work, I had the house to myself while Dad was out. Greg worked out of town that summer, and without Mom and Greg around, I didn't have to worry about fights when Dad got home drunk. I could smoke and drink with friends and not worry about Dad finding out.

I could, that is, until after a week or two, when he quit going out. And quit drinking. In the past, he'd quit for a while when he worried about Mom leaving him. But he never stayed sober for long. I wasn't celebrating. I still expected the worst so as not to be disappointed. While

Mom was gone, Dad started lingering at home, impinging on my vacation from my family.

The sun was setting and a hint of upcoming fall was in the air the night Dad walked into my room; it was the first time I could remember him ever doing that.

"How are you?" he said.

"Um. Okay." I looked at him from my seat at my eighty-year-old antique vanity, where I kept my jewelry, secret birth control pills, and diary. I was overcome by the oddity of him standing there, asking how I was. *This isn't how our relationship works.*

"Have you heard from your mother?" This was his real question, and it seemed like he had gathered courage to ask it, which made me even more uncomfortable.

"Nope." I pretended to pay close attention to how I rubbed in my face lotion.

He looked out my window, into the backyard. "Do you know why she left?"

"No. Don't you?"

He kept his gaze directed at the window, but his eyes focused much further away than the backyard, into the future or maybe the past. He remained quiet for an uncomfortable amount of time. I grabbed my brush, wanting to leave, but found myself frozen.

As if to himself, he said, "I'm wondering if she knows I've stopped drinking." And then to me, "Have you noticed a difference in me since I quit?"

I realized only then that Mom probably had left because of his drinking. I answered him honestly. "Yes. You're talking more."

Again, more silence.

"Maybe I *am* an alcoholic," he finally said.

Could it be he thought he wasn't? I raised my eyebrows when he looked at me.

"The hospital told me I had 'borderline' alcoholism." He must've been referring to the hospital he admitted himself to after France, eight years earlier.

This time it was I who was silent, flabbergasted, heart racing. Had this "borderline" bullshit kept him drinking all these years? *I* knew he was an alcoholic. It was the only explanation for him choosing to drink over being there for us, over the possibility of me having friends over, over Mom not being scared every night after he left the house, over having extra money for us.

He must have wanted to drink badly; the "borderline" diagnosis gave him the option to do so. I could hear him justifying to himself. *Borderlines can drink sometimes, right? It's not like I'm a full-blown alcoholic who needs to quit completely because I can't stop at one. Tonight, I'll stop at one.* He couldn't stop even if he wanted to. He drank until he was shit-faced and barreling through the house, breaking furniture, yelling, inevitably colliding with Mom.

"If she calls, will you tell her I'm not drinking?"

"Sure."

He couldn't live without her. But she and her illness also must have been one of the reasons he drank, because when she returned, it wasn't long before he was stumbling back into the house past midnight, ready for a fight.

· · • · ·

THOUGH KNOX COLLEGE WAS my future, each time I biked by the flourishing campus, I recoiled. Situated just one block from the town's depressed Main Street of boarded businesses, the college—shaped by strong, historic stone buildings and century-old trees and fields of green grass—stood separate and distinct from her, my run-down town that was no longer fully fed by the aboveground railroad. I wondered what went on inside those buildings on campus, buildings my father escaped to each day. The mystery intimidated me, a townie.

Living away from Broad Street sounded great, but I had zero confidence in myself as an academic. I did reasonably well in school without trying, but I knew I had not been prepared at my high school for Knox College's classes. The three of us kids considered other colleges, but Dad didn't. We would go to Knox. While I was not the superstar academic Kate was, if I managed to not get kicked out, I'd be sure to make a better impression than Greg. After delaying it for an unreasonable time, I completed the application and essay for admission to Knox College. After I received my acceptance, dread set in.

I put off packing until the day Sherry and her truck-owning boyfriend helped me move into my dorm a couple of miles away. Once I was on campus, when Dad and I saw each other, we waved subtly, as if neither of us knew if we wanted to draw attention to our connection, nor if the other person wanted to. I'd see him in the quad and the humanities building, where he had an office and I had a few classes, and we'd do our wave–not wave.

Feeling in over my head early in my first semester, I told Dad that maybe I wasn't smart enough for Knox. He replied, "You wrote a paper for admission to this school that was better written than most of what I read from my freshman students. I have no doubt you'll find something you love, and then you'll get A's. Don't worry too much about grades until then." This would prove to be the only useful advice I'd ever receive from Dad.

· · • · ·

I PLUNGED INTO MY new life with both feet and, without much thought, submerged myself in new experiences: a suite of new female friends, dancing and flirting at fraternity parties, and academics. In that order. I continued to take dumb risks, as I had since age thirteen, and, as always, never quite knew why.

In the fall of my junior year, well into my major of sociology/anthropology, I became friends with Mike. We walked out of a Cultures of Southeast Asia class together, and his flirty brown eyes caught mine. A flush of heat surged through my body as I recalled a night the year before, over winter break. He'd been on campus with his hometown friends, and we'd kissed at a small party. Our paths hadn't crossed since.

We walked side by side toward the library. With a deep voice that still cracked slightly as it likely had in adolescence, he asked to borrow my notes from a class he'd missed. He put a stick of gum in his mouth and offered me a piece.

"This anthropology part of our major is killing me," he said. I smelled the spearmint on his breath. Sunshine caught the red in his mahogany-brown hair. I noticed his crooked nose and remembered the feeling of it touching mine.

"Yeah. Me too. Sociology is way better. You can use my notes. My scribbles might not make much sense."

He laughed a laugh that invited people into his joy. His personal space was open, easy to enter, unlike students who walked within their bubbles, allowing people to get only so close. After we said goodbye, he walked toward the Beta house. His legs were lean and athletic. I resisted the physical pull, knowing Mike was a player; he was with a different girl every weekend, I'd heard. Yet I found myself easing into the rhythm of a new friendship.

Over the next couple of months, we started gathering a few of our friends and meeting weekly for "pre-socials" on nights of fraternity dance parties. It was lighthearted fun. On an early November, late-night, post-party trip to Steak 'n Shake, Mike and I returned to campus around 2:00 a.m., and it started to drizzle. He said, "I'll walk you to your dorm."

We stopped in the middle of the grassy field that separated the library from the student housing. To our east, tall lights near the tennis courts lit up mist particles around us. To our west, windows of the few students still awake in Post Hall glowed. In between, us.

I looked him in the eye, blinking away raindrops. "Why is it you call *me* to help arrange pre-parties on the weekends, but you always end up with one of my friends?" I laughed. I wanted more from him.

The rain picked up, and he pulled me into the warmth of his chest.

He lowered his chin as I moved mine up, our timing exactly right, and we kissed a kiss that left me dizzy.

"I didn't want to risk losing our friendship," he said and held me tightly.

· · • · ·

ONCE I GOT TO Knox, it wasn't long before I caught wind of Dad's reputation for missing class. But when Mike and I enrolled in Russian 101 the next trimester, with Dad as the professor, he never missed a single session of our class. As my new boyfriend, Mike also made extra effort. Eager to impress Dad, Mike studied his Russian before he studied for any other course. He quickly became a much better student than I was, and between his charisma and his Russian, Mike built a small foundation with Dad. It was subtle, like the wave–not wave between Dad and me.

I also learned soon enough that, on campus, Dad was a different person. Several older students took the time to tell me of his kindness and the way he counseled and challenged them. Students I didn't know approached me to share their stories of how he inspired and encouraged them. He changed the trajectory of their lives.

Dad's nurturing and patience, traits I hadn't known he possessed, filled me with gratification. He was the dad I had looked up to when I was that seven-year-old fingertip licker who loved his side hugs and being called *apple* and *butterball*. I wanted to be proud of him and for him to be proud of me.

I experienced some of the on-campus version of Dad too. He offered me use of his car whenever I needed it, though it meant he had to walk. I still worked at Just Pants, and the transportation helped a great deal.

One day while driving Dad's car with a friend, I took a left turn in the rain and slammed into a car I didn't see coming. The merciless driver screamed accusations and left me shaken. I walked with my ticket from the accident to Dad's office. When I got there, I stood at his door, wet from the rain. With a red face and eyes swollen from crying, I said, "Dad, I was in an accident. It was my fault, and I totaled your car; it's not even drivable."

He opened his arms, hugged me, and said, "I can always replace the car. I can't replace my daughter." He was a different person. On campus and without Mom.

11

HARM!

YELLOW STICKY NOTES COVERED with the words *Harm!*, *Danger!*, or illegible smudges grew like weeds throughout my parents' house. At first, during my junior year in college, I only saw two or three stuck to the kitchen cabinets whenever I visited Mom. On subsequent visits, I noticed dozens upon dozens of these notes invading like a climbing ivy, crawling up the kitchen cupboards, or on open books scattered around the coffee table, the couch, and the dining room table. Yet asking Mom about the encroachment meant tending the garden, work that required a special skill or a talent, something our family didn't have. Instead, we'd learned to ignore this invasive species whose tendrils clung tightly.

During one visit, Mom paced in front of the counters, moved a dish and put it back in the same spot, and turned her head to the side and then dropped it to her chest again. Her lips moved and inflections punctuated the sound of her voice, but I couldn't make out full sentences.

"Who are you talking to, Mom?"

On the defensive, she replied, "It's quite normal to talk to yourself! Aunt Hilda does it too."

Living on campus just a couple of miles from home made it hard for me to not stop by on occasion. I felt the obligation to be a daughter who shows up and the guilt that came if I didn't. Afterward, I would recharge by spending time at a bar with friends. Whenever the topic of Mom came up, I'd say she was tired and weird. I'd say she was driving me nuts. Maybe I'd go ahead and just let it out: "My mom is crazy!" And someone might say, "Duh, yeah! My mom's crazy too." I never knew where to go from there. Other kids thought their moms were crazy because they made them eat dinner at a certain time, wouldn't let them stay out late, or put fruit in their Jell-O. I knew better.

· · • · ·

KATE CAME HOME FOR Christmas that year, my junior year at Knox. She had eloped with her college boyfriend, Brian, and they lived in Rockford, Illinois, a couple of hours away. They walked into the house on Broad Street on Christmas Eve, and I saw Mom from their perspective. With her hair poking out in different directions, she'd opened the door for them, narrowed her eyes, and frowned. Kate may have been expecting to be turned away. The last time she'd come to visit from Rockford, Mom had told her to leave; she didn't want to see her. This time, Mom let them in. The house was dark and cold, like an empty icebox. When Mom spoke she didn't make sense. She mentioned she wasn't cooking dinner, and she went to her room.

For the first year ever, there was no Christmas tree.

Kate, Brian, and I left. We ate five-dollar meals at an Alfano's Pizzeria and laughed while slurping down greasy mozzarella and red sauce, thinking that it might be the best Christmas Eve ever. Kate and Brian stayed with a friend and came to the house the next day. I don't know where Greg was.

"How's it going?" Kate asked.

"Oh, just peachy. I'm so glad you guys are here. Merry Christmas."

"Merry Christmas," Kate said back. We said "Merry Christmas" to the tune of "my condolences."

Later that day, Kate told me she had seen Mom wearing her mysterious black eye patch.

"What's the eye patch for?" she had asked her. "Are your eyes okay?"

"I think you know, so I'm not going to tell you," Mom had said.

Kate, a nutrition expert, was concerned by Mom's dramatic weight loss, so she'd pushed on that topic instead. Mom expressed fear about what was in food—the fat and the additives and "who knows what." Her baggy clothes and gaunt face told us she didn't eat much of anything anymore.

"I can't find certain things. They've been taken," she told Kate.

"What are you missing, Mom?"

"My thoughts, for one!" she yelled, and Kate backed off.

Kate, having the benefits of living in a larger town and working in health care, knew more now about what might be going on with Mom and how to get her help. Once she was back home in Rockford, Kate did some research and found a referral for a psychiatrist. She told him about Mom and made an appointment at a medical center in Peoria, about forty minutes away from Galesburg. She called my dorm, and together we devised a scheme to get Mom to the appointment.

Kate called Dad to get his approval and his agreement to come with us. He knew Kate was right; he said he would come along to the appointment if Mom agreed to go, but he wouldn't be there when we talked with Mom about the appointment. We decided to tell Greg afterward, as we couldn't risk having an adversary. Kate and I worried he might work against us, as he'd begun to do more and more. We'd each started to feel like his rival in any interaction we had with him. This effort was bound to trigger his stance of opposition.

· · • · ·

AS WAS USUAL BY this time, I woke up next to Mike and to the familiar smells of his fraternity house—stale beer and aftershave. We made love on his full-size mattress, which he'd placed directly on the floor and took up most of his room.

It was the day my sister's plan was to come together. Stoic, I mentioned this to Mike. He took my face in his hands and said, "I know it's gonna be a hard day for you, Izzie. I'll be thinking of you."

I had kept most of the Mom part of my life tucked away from him, and me, and everyone. Yet Mike knew enough to feel a bit of what I was feeling. We spent all our free time together, but it was still early in our relationship—just over three months since our kiss in the rain. Unwilling to accept platitudes, he'd been the first person to insist I try to explain my feelings, insisting that they mattered. It was painful, but I was beginning for the first time, at age twenty, to understand and tell the difference between my emotions of anger, envy, frustration, sadness. Putting words to feelings. Naming them. This helped me separate enough from my emotions to be able to assess how to handle them, so they wouldn't prompt unhealthy actions. This is a skill every child should be taught before they grow up and raise children.

Later that morning, I walked the path to George Davis Hall, where I took my sociology class and where Dad also had a second-floor office. For over three years, I'd walked this same path, yet no other time do I remember like this one.

Once inside the building, I struggled to pick up my feet as I took the stairs. Would I see Dad? Would we see dread in each other's eyes? We wouldn't talk, I knew this. I poked my head into his office. Empty. I let out a breath.

I found a seat in my classroom down the hall and arranged myself, trying and failing to connect my brain to the world around me. The other students chatted about the reading, the weekend, normal things. I focused on the outdoors. The window framed a familiar view:

century-old brick buildings surrounded by large expanses of grass, towering oaks, and weeping willows.

My fingertips felt dry, and I licked them. I hadn't felt the need to lick my fingertips since I was nine years old. *Kate must be in town by now*, I thought. I was nervous, but maybe not as nervous as I should've been. Accepting Kate's direction and control, I refused, in honed survival mode, to fully anticipate all the possibilities. Ahead lay a big day for our family, for Mom.

Our plan included deceit, and my stomach clenched with the betrayal. I felt protective of Mom, of her dignity, but I also had developed a deep desire for truth after a childhood of obfuscations. We'd decided to tell Mom we were worried about her and Dad, and we wanted them to see a psychologist, a marriage counselor. Our appointment was actually with a hospital psychiatrist. This was the best way, the only way, we told ourselves, to get her the help she needed.

Kate picked me up after class, and we drove in silence the short distance to the house. If Mom agreed, we'd call Dad and tell him it was time to go.

I started to anticipate Mom's reaction. She got angry fast in those days. I didn't feel a mother's love, though I'd yearned for it, yet I was full of concern for her. The mother-daughter bond was like an unspoken oath, a pledge for me to not do harm, to try to make her proud, and it was a promise of loyalty. She feared people doing her harm and people conspiring against her. She'd interpret our intervention as conspiracy to do harm, and I knew it.

When Mom was angry, both Kate and I cowered and crept away; never did we stay and fight. Today, we'd need to stay. We'd need to keep pushing. Keep moving forward toward our goal of getting her help.

12

A DIAGNOSIS

KATE AND I RANG the doorbell since Mom wasn't expecting us. Mom opened the red door of our gray stucco family home without expression. I noticed her clothes—an old shirt and clashing pants that were held up with a belt from another outfit. This, her pasty skin, and her messy, frizzy hair told me we were doing the right thing.

"Hi. What have you been up to this morning?" I asked as we stood in the foyer.

I imagined her wearing her eye patch, jogging in loops around the basement. Perhaps she'd spent the hours looking up words in her dictionaries and making notations on Post-it notes.

She studied me for a moment, then looked away. "If you don't already know, I think it's best if I keep it to myself."

"How would we already know?" I asked, trying to keep my voice lighthearted. "We just got here, and Kate just got into town."

Mom squinted and tensed her jaw.

Kate asked, "What do you think of this weather?"

"Mmmm. I haven't been out," Mom said. She pulled her shoulders back, looked down, and tightened her belt.

We walked through the dining room to the living room, and I noticed Mom or Dad had attempted some do-it-yourself interior design work. The 1920s moldings, trim, and plaster walls all had received a coat of fresh, asylum-white paint. With a flat finish. The room contained an odd mix of furniture: inherited old English Victorian and early 1970s American. Mom's treasured Oriental rug lay beneath it all like a fine porcelain platter presenting a stack of stale mixed crackers. Across the rug, she had laid a three-foot-wide stretch of transparent plastic to protect it from foot traffic.

When we sat down, my insides were the mangled metal of a train wreck. I looked toward the front windows. The blinds were closed, as they always were, to keep Mom's thoughts from being stolen.

"Why are you here?" Mom said. Her lips landed in a flat line.

Kate's voice shook a little as she leaned forward in her chair. "Mom, Liz and I are here because we're worried about you. About you and Dad." She spoke slowly, with her bottom lip kept firm so as not to quiver.

Mom frowned, furrowing her eyebrows as she moved her chin down toward her neck. "I don't know what you're talking about." She spoke fast.

Kate's chest rose and fell, but she stuck to her stance of thoughtful concern. "When I was here at Christmas, I felt like you were very unhappy and that you might want help."

We weren't prepared to ask, *Why do you leave crazy notes of danger around the house and talk to people who aren't visible to us? Why do you think people read your thoughts and broadcast them to the world?* We pretended it was a normal conversation about a normal couple having marriage issues. It was the only way we could do this. We weren't mental health professionals, and we didn't want her to lash out or distrust us. We'd never get her to the psychiatrist then. Even today, with her disheveled appearance, she kept her head high and led with obstinacy. We each had our survival techniques.

It was my turn to speak up. "We are worried you might be depressed and that you aren't happy in your marriage. We'd like you and Dad to get help." I managed to get that much out with a voice shakier than Kate's.

Mom leaned forward, relaxed her facial muscles, and engaged eyes with us. Our moment had arrived, and I felt the full weight of it. Maybe it was far-fetched, but because of Kate—her initiative to research mental illness, talk with a psychiatrist, and make an appointment—there now existed a small possibility to get Mom the help that could turn her into a different mother, a happier mother. I sat frozen, unable to move. My elbows dug into my waist; my hands sat folded, white-knuckled, on my lap.

Encouraged by Mom's visible interest, Kate said, "As your daughters, we find it hard to see you and Dad this way. It makes it hard for us to visit. I made a special trip to talk with you and see if you'll come with us and with Dad to see a psychologist. Dad's already agreed." It sounded rehearsed because it was.

Mom fell back into her seat, her body softened. We sat still for a minute. My heart pounded in my throat.

And then, to our surprise, she said, "Okay. Your father sought help on a few occasions. Perhaps it's my turn. I can do the same." Everything with Dad was a competition for her; everything had to be fair, though her mind would rarely let her see things as such. She typically fought against any idea that wasn't hers, for fear of maltreatment. We were stunned and briefly relieved.

Kate and I had cleared our first hurdle for the day. But we didn't let down our guard. The hard part was yet to come. Kate called Dad to let him know he should meet us at the house, that we'd be driving to Peoria and continuing with the plan.

We waited, still anxious, while Mom went upstairs to get ready to go.

We knew Mom would catch on to our ruse at some point. She wouldn't acknowledge her illness directly, and we'd lose all her trust if we did. Kate had learned before coming to town that since Mom wasn't a danger to herself or others, we couldn't force her to get help; she had to be willing. Our next hurdle would be significantly higher.

・ ・ ● ・ ・

WE TOOK SEPARATE CARS to the hospital. Mom rode with Kate, and Dad and I followed in Dad's car, in silence. I rested my head against the window. Clouds and mist created a dreamscape: the sky, the air, the road—all just different shades of gray.

At the hospital, people stood shoulder to shoulder in the waiting room, silent or speaking in muffled tones. Mom and Dad stood apart from each other along the wall. Dad looked into space, and Mom moved her lips like she was talking, but I couldn't hear words. It seemed odd for it to be as crowded as it was, like there was some public health crisis causing everyone to seek treatment at once. I'd expected a calm, private situation, but the air was thick with a silent intensity. People in some stage of mental or physical breakdown and their family members, standing around with their coats over their arms, wore pained expressions of uncertainty and anticipation.

Transparent glass surrounded the waiting room. I remember thinking this would be tough for those who thought people were watching them. Then again, I suppose it was important for the professionals on the outside of the room to be able to view the status of the waiting room by glancing over. The carpet and the chairs were variations of gray, the motif of the day.

The heart of the waiting room was a large reception desk. Several people leaned there for support. We found a couple of seats and gave them to Mom and Dad, who were still and rigid. Kate and I stood and blended in with the other relatives who were questioning their decisions and the future.

Just as I started to settle in, Mom pointed to a speaker embedded in a ceiling panel. "Do you hear what they are saying?" She didn't wait for an answer. "That song, those voices. I can't quite make it out. Wait. Shhhhh! Okay, they're repeating it over and over. Do you hear it? It's telling me to do something time after time."

Mom's face tightened, and her eyes darted, lizard-like, as she worked to make out the words in Cyndi Lauper's song. Kate and I looked at each other. If we'd been unsure about bringing Mom to get help, those doubts faded with every word she uttered.

What is taking so long?

Rapid-fire, Mom rattled off a string of associations. "Time after time. Time and time again. A stitch in time. There's no time like the present. Hurry, now, there's no time to lose. I'm having the time of my life." She gasped and laughed an angry laugh. She wasn't talking to us or to anyone we could see. *Will the doctor please see us now?*

Finally, a nurse called our name and escorted us into the doctor's office. The color palette changed to shades of brown. In between two rough-fabric chairs and a couch sat a tan, rectangular coffee table. The walls were beige, as was a swivel stool chair positioned across from the couch. There was an oddly situated post in the middle of the room that separated one of the chairs from a worktable. In the land of the misfit furniture and design, we stood waiting.

Dr. Andrews opened the door and walked briskly into the room. He was short in stature, with dark hair and dark eyes. "I'm sorry for the wait. Please sit down."

He looked at Mom and Dad. "Your daughter Kate and I spoke on the phone, and I'd like to be sure we agree as to why we're here. She said she and your daughter Liz are worried about your happiness and your marriage and thought you might benefit from counseling. They're particularly concerned about you, Cathryn. They've noticed your weight loss and worry you're depressed. Do I have this right, Kate and Liz?"

Certain my body's vibrations might lift me off the itchy, brown couch, I felt myself nodding. My jaw locked, but I managed to mumble something confirming my support for his version of events. Kate responded with real words but also visibly and audibly trembled. We weren't raised to do this sort of thing. Neither our genetic makeup nor our in-house training had prepared us to seek solutions to complex, sensitive problems. Our family comfort zone was the size of a US nickel, and we were fumbling around with hefty amounts of a foreign currency. What were we doing here?

Dr. Andrews swiveled from person to person to face whomever he was speaking. It wasn't long before he focused on Mom, who was clearly the patient. He asked her a long series of questions, and she answered them curtly. No, she doesn't sleep well. Yes, she's a bit tired. No, her marriage isn't going well. No, she doesn't think she worries any more than anyone else. No, she'd rather not say if she feels depressed. Then she pointed at Dad. "Why aren't you asking *him* any questions?"

He asked Dad just a few yes-or-no questions related to his perception of Mom's behaviors and his interest in helping her and their marriage. Yes, he saw her as depressed. No, he didn't know how to help her. Yes, he wanted his marriage to work. Yes, he would work on it with her.

I recalled the last time we were in a doctor's office together. Twelve years had passed since the psychologist's office in Seattle, after we fled France without Dad. That time, nothing came of it. This time, Kate was in charge. This time, we might create positive change.

Dr. Andrews asked Mom, "What are you feeling right now?"

"What am I feeling? I feel like I don't know what's going on here." She rose out of her seat and then, like she knew she had nowhere to go, sat down again.

"What is it you're concerned about?" he asked, pen in hand, ready to take notes.

"This. What is this? Are we going to talk about his drinking?" She pointed at Dad again.

I thought it was a good question, but I also knew we weren't there for Dad.

Dr. Andrews swiveled a bit in his chair and then faced Mom again. "We want to focus on you now. Your daughters are concerned about you."

Mom rose again and walked around the room. She was mad, but no longer psychotic mad. She wasn't talking with people we couldn't see or responding to messages from the speakers. She was answering questions and trying to escape. Her actions and words seemed rational.

My heart ached for her. We'd railroaded her, and I suddenly wanted to jump up and push her from the tracks, protect her from the oncoming locomotive, protect her pride, be the loyal daughter she'd hoped for. I'd learned to put up walls to protect myself, and now I had the urge to protect her, give her the security I longed for. We'd ganged up, lied. I couldn't imagine how it felt to be her, but she was my mom, and I no longer was certain we were doing the right thing.

Dr. Andrews cleared his throat. "Cathy, would you please come back to the conversation? We want to hear your opinion."

Mom eyed Dr. Andrews warily. She made her way back to her chair but didn't sit.

Dr. Andrews stepped toward Mom. "Cathy, I have an important question for you: Would you be willing to stay at the hospital to get the help that might make you feel better?"

The big question was out there. Sweat flooded my quivering hands.

Mom heaved a sigh of exhaust and angst, grabbed her purse, and walked toward the door before stopping short. "I don't want to lose access to my finances," she said. "If I do this, if I agree to stay, will I lose my financial independence?"

"No, Cathy," the doctor said. "You won't lose your rights if you choose to get help on your own. If your family arranges it so you end up staying here against your will, then you might lose your financial independence."

Mom locked eyes with Kate.

Without hesitation, Kate said, "Yes, Mom, if you don't do this on your own, I'll try to get you help any way I can."

Mom tightened her lips and pulled her chin to her neck. "Well then. If it'll allow me to keep my finances, then yes, I'll stay."

I'd like to say I felt relief at that moment, and maybe I did. But I was fried, nerves dulled, and ready for a beer and a cigarette.

· · • · ·

SINCE THERE WASN'T A room available for Mom in the psychiatric ward until the next day, Mom and Kate stayed overnight at the general hospital, though neither slept. Dad drove me back to campus. It was a forty-five-minute drive, yet following family form, we at first rode in silence.

After fifteen miles, Dad spoke. "I've been trying to recall when your mother's illness might've started." He spoke to the highway, not me.

He stared at the road. Our drive was a straight shot, but he looked lost.

"I've wondered that too," I said.

He held the wheel with his left hand, and with his right, he rubbed his mustache for a while. "I don't know. She's said and done strange things since her late twenties. Yes. She might've been struggling with this since then."

Oh my god. I couldn't look at him. I stared out at the darkening gunmetal-gray day until he dropped me off at my dorm and we said bye because there was nothing else either of us could say.

· · • · ·

MOM SPENT ONE MONTH at the hospital. Dad told us she pretended to take her medication the first five days. No one noticed until it didn't show up in a urine sample. The health care staff watched her after that. The doctors were beginning to diagnose her situation. But after the fourth week, Mom called Dad and convinced him to take her home.

The doctor told Dad that Mom had schizoaffective disorder, a serious and persistent mental illness that combines schizophrenia—where people experience distorted views of reality, delusions, hallucinations, and disorganized thinking—and a mood disorder such as depression.

Our hope was that she would continue getting care on an outpatient basis and that she'd find the medications helpful. We had to believe that all the effort, all the emotional strain, would at least give us a mom who acknowledged her illness and took steps to control it.

The side effects of the antipsychotic drug, which for Mom included cotton mouth and some involuntary motor movements, Dad told us, were intolerable for her. After a few more weeks, she decided to stop taking her meds, and Dad supported her decision.

"She's very uncomfortable," Dad said. He sounded so certain of the choice, I sensed he was justifying the decision, that he knew the news would flatten us. But we heard relief in his voice. Kate and I both surmised that he'd not liked having his wife in the hospital, the expense of it, and he didn't like her complaining about the side effects of the medication.

Kate was living in Rockford, and I was on campus. We didn't know what her symptoms looked like, and we weren't privy to the conversations Mom and Dad had about her treatment. As far as we know, they didn't try different doses or investigate the new antipsychotic medications that were developed and marketed in later years. Medications for her illness were difficult to get right because everyone's different, and the disease impacts each person in a unique way. Many people on medication for mental illness try different kinds and doses before arriving at the optimal pharmaceutical situation. Not our parents.

It was over. No longer a topic of discussion. When that term, *schizoaffective disorder*, left the doctor's mouth, it evaporated, disappeared, and we all resigned ourselves to forgetting it, or at least to turning the other way again. She resisted treatment and didn't acknowledge her illness, so how could we? With quiet voices, when required to say something, we said, "Our mom has mental health issues." And the elephant hunkered down, reestablishing his residence right in the middle of our goddamn symmetrical home.

We'd won the battle but lost the war. Exhausted and deflated, Kate went back to work in Rockford, and I finished the spring term at Knox. I blamed Dad for giving up, but we didn't talk about these things. He was still my default role model for communications, and I followed his lead. My view was that he wasn't strong enough, he wasn't brave enough, and in predictable form, he'd surrendered.

New research suggests an increase in schizophrenia spectrum illnesses. They are thought to occur in approximately 0.5–1.8 percent of people at some point in their lives. Such an illness can last weeks or months and then go into remission. Alternatively, it may never abate, or it may do something in between. The range of how it manifests differs by individual as well. For Mom, it seemed to always be there, never life-threatening but never completely gone either.

While we claimed our mom did not acknowledge or that she denied her illness, I learned later in my life that schizophrenia has a common neurological symptom wherein the individual is unaware of their illness. It's called anosognosia. It's hard for caregivers and family members to understand, and it's a serious obstacle to getting people with schizophrenia treatment.

· · • · ·

OVER THE NEXT FEW years, Mom declined even further. She became thinner and more antisocial. She cut off contact with the one or two friends left in her life and stayed in the house. Her detachment, delusions, and hallucinations continued. Her face was grim. When conversations with her moved into bizarro land, she'd either get angry or simply stop talking once she realized, maybe because of our looks of disbelief, that our reality differed from hers.

At the same time, her lucid brain took on a new role of vigilance: she wasn't interested in receiving "help" again, and she kept careful guard against any perceived interference on our part.

Our aunt Carol and great-aunt Hilda, who were both in fine mental health, expressed anger at our efforts. Kate got the calls from each of them after we took Mom to the hospital; despite hearing details of Mom's decline, their message was, "How could you have done this to Cathy? Your mom! She doesn't need medication or a doctor! Maybe she's tired or sad from your dad's drinking. Nothing that a little love and attention from her daughters can't cure."

A monster, the stigma of mental illness, cornered even those who cared most about Mom. That well-fed monster spread misinformation, ignorance, and inertia, smothering any hope we might have had and any hope for Mom.

13

CHRISTMAS

THE MONTHS BEFORE MY senior year of college, I worked my third summer in a row in a great-paying job at Butler Manufacturing as a laborer. At my year-round Fannie May candies mall job, I wore a blue smock and hairnet, but at Butler, I donned heavy, leather steel-toed boots, a "Butler Blue" plastic hard hat, and safety glasses. I felt strong as I plodded across cement floors, lifted steel parts, and tolerated noisy machinery and men leering and hooting. I was a member of the United Steelworkers union, thank you very much, sweltering in the heat and humidity of some of the hottest days on record, inside a factory with men of all sorts, including—almost always on the same shift as I was—a bear-size, cigar-chewing man with no teeth, nicknamed "Tiny."

After each week of labor, on Fridays, I'd get off my shift, full of sweat and dirt, and Mike would be waiting for me. Sometimes I'd work second shift and I'd be walking out of the factory at 11:30 p.m. Still, Mike stood next to his early 1980s maroon Oldsmobile Cutlass Supreme, watching for me to walk out with all the middle-aged men. He'd drive down three hours to get me and wait in the parking lot, and we'd drive back three hours to his town.

Our weekends in rural northern Illinois were spent at his dad's air-conditioned trailer or with his mom—I called her Sandy-Mom—and her husband. Mike's hometown friends welcomed me into the clan. Life became our amusement park, and we rode in Mike's car, sunroof open, soaking in the warmth, smelling the ripening corn from the fields, hanging our bare feet out the window, listening to John Mellencamp, Van Halen, and Lynyrd Skynyrd. We sang along at the top of our lungs as we took sharp corners at great speeds. One of Mike's favorite songs was "Pink Houses" by Mellencamp. We'd turn the volume up for that one. I loved to hear Mike's deep, crusty voice duetting with Mellencamp. We drank beers, swam in lakes, and played beach volleyball in the blistering heat.

Beer, beef, and belly-aching laughter were the staples at any gathering of Mike's extended family, where they celebrated and comforted one another. They argued, got angry, and made up, ready to do it again. Mike always wanted me to talk things out, risk a fight, not clam up or flee. His approach to conflict was an extension of his family's. As was mine. But he was making progress with me, encouraging me to stand up for myself, to express myself.

Mike's family more than accepted me, but I was a cultural anthropologist in their world, observing them from the fringe. Their ease with one another made me uncomfortable. I wanted them to like me so much that I smiled a lot and was agreeable on all counts. I'd been using this social approach for so long because I didn't know any other way. It turned out to be a lonely and stressful approach. I hadn't yet created many strong opinions, but my body had, and it shared them with me, through stomachaches mostly.

I didn't want to lose this possible family of what I considered "normal" people. I wanted them to like me. I had pretended so much, my whole life, that I didn't know who I was. How could I join this group of genuine, lively people?

· · • · ·

FALL TERM. EIGHT MONTHS had passed since our scheming to get Mom to the hospital, then learning of her diagnosis, only to have it change nothing.

As school got underway my senior year, Greg, still at Knox, cheated on his girlfriend, Teri, someone I considered a friend. Greg bragged about his womanizing. He took Teri's hard-earned money, bought drugs with it, and had her drive him to fraternity parties where he hit on other women.

On a Mississippi riverboat cruise sponsored by Mike's fraternity, I asked Mike if he thought I should tell Teri. This felt big for me. The idea of speaking a truth that could deeply hurt someone I cared about, even if I hoped to help, was wrought with pain. It wasn't something I'd considered doing since the first time I had done so with Mom and the psychiatrist. Since he was a guy, and someone who'd played many fields before dating me, I was interested in Mike's perspective.

On the deck of the boat, what had been a warm September day turned into a chilly night. Mike wrapped his light-blue blazer over my padded shoulders. His brown eyes fastened onto mine. "This is the way I see it, Izzie: once a guy is with a girl he's really into, he wants to spend all his time with her, and he stops messing around. He doesn't want to screw it up."

"So, I should tell her?" I shivered, and the wind grabbed my crisp, hair-sprayed bangs and moved them up in one horizontal plane.

He sighed. "I'm saying I just don't think this is the girl for Greg. But you gotta do what you think you need to." He faced me, put his arms around my waist, under his suit jacket. His rough voice whispered, "I haven't wanted to hang out with anyone but you for a long time. It's been ten months."

I pulled away from his chest. "Me neither. And that must be a record for you!"

He smiled, reached into his suit pocket, and pulled out a little black box.

"Izzie, I brought my fraternity pin. I want you to wear it, or not, but I want you to have it. If you take it, it's supposed to mean we're pre-engaged."

My heart lifted as he placed the box in my hands. Inside was a half-inch gold-and-black pin shaped like a tiny police badge. Embedded in its center was a gold laurel wreath with a diamond inside, like an egg in a gilded nest.

Being with Mike meant warmth and excitement. It meant comfort and thrills, family and friends. It meant having someone who saw into me and wanted my commitment and loyalty.

I took his pin, and I knew that I had to tell Teri about Greg.

· · • · ·

I EXPECTED ANGER AND pain from Teri; that's how I'd respond. So I gathered my thoughts and courage and called her from my college apartment phone.

"Teri. This is going to be hard for you to hear." My voice was shaky. "I'm sorry. I wouldn't be telling you if I hadn't thought about it a lot."

"Liz! What's going on?"

"Greg's been sleeping around. I know he's been with a few women at Knox. One he's been seeing a lot."

Teri was quiet. "Oh. How do you know for sure?"

"I know her. And Greg doesn't hide it. I'm so sorry. I didn't think you should be the last to know."

"I'll talk to Greg." She sounded stronger.

"He'll deny it, you know. If you need to—I don't want you to, but if you need to—you can tell him it was me. That you found out from me."

"Thanks, Liz . . . I gotta go." She hung up.

A week later, when she confronted Greg, he reframed the situation, denied it, blamed her, and then somehow charmed his way out of the truth. When I talked with her on the phone after she talked with Greg, she wasn't angry with me, as I'd half expected. She said she loved him and wanted to believe him, so she was going to stay with him. She hadn't told him I'd told her. I wondered when he'd find out who the messenger had been.

· · • · ·

INSTEAD OF GOING HOME for the Christmas holiday break, I was thrilled to be able to stay at the apartment I shared with three college friends, just a couple of miles away. My roommates, conversely, were excited to go home to their families. I had the place to myself.

Mike headed home a week before Christmas, and I sold chocolates the busiest days of the year at Fannie May. I planned to head north on Christmas Eve to spend the holiday with Mike and his family. I had picked out his present, a sweater he'd never wear.

As I packed my travel bag on Christmas Eve morning, I looked out the sliding glass windows of our balcony and saw my brother and Teri walking up to the building. I was surprised because they never stopped by. My heart pounded. I looked around and realized there was no escape, no back door. I'd anticipated an eventual confrontation with Greg, and now it was coming. I paced the small apartment, and my stomach turned.

When I answered the door, the first thing I noticed was their grim faces. They came into my living room, quiet and solemn. We sat on the couch, each of us a bit stiff and shaky. I got a whiff of Greg's leather jacket.

I decided to stand firm. I'd done the right thing by telling Teri; now, if she decided to marry him and he became a cheating husband, I would have a clear conscience. I was so busy preparing my response, I initially failed to realize that Greg looked terrified.

Fumbling with his unlit cigarette, he looked at me and said, "Liz, I don't know how to say this . . . Mike's mom called the house, and I answered. Mike was in a serious car accident." His gray-blue eyes searched mine for a sign I'd understood what he said.

"What? Where is he? How is he?" I took a deep breath, stood up, and walked around to try to fill my lungs. I visualized a hospital scene with broken legs, a ventilator, flowers all around, me sitting with Mike and reading a book to him.

Still looking at me, statue still, he said, "Liz, uh, I'm sorry. Man, this is hard. Mike didn't make it, and neither did his friend. I, uh, guess they were hit by a semitruck and died at the scene."

I fell against a wall, slid to the floor, and screamed an elongated "No!" When I finally stopped to take a breath, I couldn't. I heaved.

Mike, who had chipped away at my buffers, had insisted I put words to my feelings, whose affection I craved, was dead. I would never touch him again. Gone were his brown eyes and his giant laugh. Gone was his future, our future.

Later that day, I called Mike's mom, my Sandy-Mom. She told me she hadn't wanted to call me where she knew I was alone. She asked me to please consider still coming to be with her family over the holidays, for the funeral.

Her firstborn son had died. And she hadn't wanted me to be alone when I heard.

· • ● • ·

LATER THAT DAY, KATE, Brian, and I entered my parents' house. In the cold, empty foyer near where the Christmas tree normally would've been, we stood wondering where our parents were.

Dad looked down as he walked up from behind us to mumble, "It's really awful . . . about Mike."

Mom was in the kitchen, where nothing was cooking. She knew we were there, but it took her a minute before she walked slowly into the dining room toward the foyer. She stopped across the room from us.

Breathing deeply, still trembling, I felt thankful for what years of disillusionment had taught me: keep expectations low and move on, fast.

We stood quiet and awkward for a few moments. Recognizing that the sudden death of their daughter's boyfriend hadn't changed them, I said, "Okay. Well, Kate and Brian offered to drive me early to Mike's family in Mt. Morris. We wanted to say goodbye."

At those words, Dad hugged Kate and me, then reached out and shook Brian's hand and wished him a merry Christmas. I walked up to Mom, who still stood a good distance away: diminutive and retiring, yet commanding the sterile and stifling aura of the room. I hugged her. She limp-noodle hugged me. I backed away.

Kate stepped forward for her hug. Mom dropped her arms and let them hang at her side as Kate embraced her. It had been less than a year since Kate and I had convinced her to go to the hospital. She still placed the blame squarely on Kate.

I felt grief well up in my chest and flip to anger. "Mom, Mike just died! His mother just lost a child. And you can't hug your daughter?" I yelled.

She stared at me without answering. I couldn't believe it. At the earliest stages of my grief, I'd shown my fury and still received nothing close to a normal response.

I grabbed Kate and marched out of the house.

14

GRADUATION

MIKE'S DEATH CHANGED EVERYTHING for me and nothing for most of the rest of the world. I learned firsthand how anyone could die or experience a loved one's death at any time. It didn't matter where you lived or how old you were. Without your consent, you could wake up to a new, almost blank-page future, or not wake up at all.

Mike, force of energy that he was, managed to stay alive in my dreams. In each one, he was enthusiastic, living a different life. He had amnesia, he was in a federal protection program; it was all in my imagination, or it was all fake—he hadn't died. In some, the most painful, he didn't think about contacting me. These dreams were punishing roller coasters that had me elated one moment, then crushed me the next. I'd wake up soaking wet from tears or sweat, wiped out, and arrested by the reality that he was, in fact, gone forever.

I had spent Christmas break with Mike's family, protected by shared grief and love. His family took me in, cared for me. As we planned Mike's funeral together, Sandy-Mom asked if I'd give Mike's fraternity pin, my pre-engagement pin, to the undertaker to put on Mike's lapel.

I hesitated to let go of this token of our love, but she had asked nothing else of me, and she had given everything. My parents never inquired about the funeral service or how they might be able to help; I had never thought they might.

Back at Knox College in January, less than a month after Mike's death, many people had no idea what to say to me. I didn't blame them; I wouldn't have known either. I walked around campus in a daze, going through the motions of a normal life. I felt I had a giant X on my sweater that told people to feel sorry for me. I hated that. While feeling weak and broken, I did my best to project strength. It's what I thought I should do, for myself and for others.

At a bar after the on-campus memorial held for Mike, a friend of his from freshman year approached me. John, with sandy-brown hair and a voice that was somehow both gravelly and smooth, had a compelling blend of thoughtful intelligence and athleticism. It was a small school, so I knew him, but not well.

"Can you introduce me to Mike's mom? I want to tell her what an amazing woman I think she is."

His direct approach knocked me out of my grief trance. He didn't look at me with pity or unease. Instead, his focus was on someone else.

I made the introduction and watched from across the loud, smoky room. I noticed Sandy-Mom's brown curls and grief-worn face. She smiled and wept as she listened to John tell his stories about Mike. Their heads touched so they could hear each other over the noise.

Later that night, unable to sleep, I knocked on the door of John's apartment, just down the hall from mine, to see how he thought his talk with Sandy had gone. He invited me in. We walked out onto his balcony and stood, on an unseasonably warm January evening, taking in the dark campus, the bright moon.

"It's so hard to imagine what it would be like to lose a child," John said. He spoke as if he were decades older than he was.

I tried to breathe the night air, the air I used to share with Mike, into my tired chest. "How do you think Sandy is doing?"

"She seems strong. I told her about me and Mike spending time together freshman year, when we first came to school for summer football practice."

I nodded and wrapped my arms around myself.

"How are you doing?" His eyes looked back and forth at mine like he was trying to see inside.

I started to lie, say I was fine, but went with the truth: "It's like I'm going through the motions of life, but I can't sleep, and when I do, I have these crushing dreams about Mike. Like he's not really dead but he's decided to live a life without me."

John put his arm around me and gave me a side hug as we walked back into his apartment. He was attractive in a way that would've made me nervous under normal circumstances. Broad shoulders, hazel eyes, and soft, pink lips. He took his time in conversation, considering every word before he said it and listening intently. He was unlike anyone I'd met—though he reminded me a bit of my sister's husband, Brian, whom I'd always admired. Confident and strong, yet sensitive and perceptive.

Exhausted, I dropped to his bed and stared at his ceiling. He positioned himself next to me, staring up as well.

"Close your eyes," he said.

I drew in a deep breath, and my eyes fluttered shut.

"Imagine a farm on a cool, crisp day. It's quiet except for the soft wind rustling through the golden fields of corn ready for harvest. You are next to a quiet lake, and you take off your shoes. Dipping your toes in, you feel the fresh, clear water as you swirl them around, making ripples on the surface. Hear the loon, smell the pine."

His skin smelled sweet and earthy, like chamomile. I pictured the scene, heard the wind, felt the calm. My eyelids stopped fluttering. I suspected these were imaginings that gave him peace too. I fell asleep while he was midsentence and woke with the warmth of the sun on my cheek.

We fell into a pattern. I'd limp my way through each day zombified by grief before entering his room near midnight. We'd lie holding each other, sometimes until dawn. It felt so good, the reprieve from the gutted ache of loss, that I pushed away any idea of our togetherness being wrong. Nothing else mattered. Who was the final judge of how best to grieve anyway?

Then people began to talk. Mike and John were in the same fraternity, and some brothers approached John. Our relationship was wrong, they said. They said I was vulnerable, John should know better, that Mike had only just died.

Within a couple of months after our first night together, John realized he couldn't reconcile our ill-timed affection. He wrote me a letter that I didn't understand, though I knew his resolve. He thought we should no longer see each other. Whatever we had wasn't good for either of us.

The afternoon I got his letter, I went to his apartment. We sat on his bed, facing each other. I started sweating. I could tell by his body language, by the way he sought the right words and came up short, that he'd changed. We'd changed. Everything had changed. He tried to explain but spoke in circles, and I couldn't absorb his words. In my disbelief, I tried to make sense of what he said but could not form thoughts to speak. I left in shock.

His intentions were sound. We couldn't move forward together, but I hadn't thought ahead more than a day. He stopped speaking to me, and his sudden absence broke me further, beyond the wreck I had been before he began to fix me with his words, body, and chamomile smell.

Deep down, I knew he was right; our timing was wrong. But the loss was too much. I sank into a deeper grief for Mike, one now mired with self-reproach.

· · • · ·

SANDY-MOM AND HER HUSBAND, George, traveled to Galesburg to attend my college graduation ceremony, held indoors due to heavy rain. Dad, less than two miles away, didn't come. He said he had a cold. His colleagues sat onstage in their velvet robes and on their folding chairs; Dad's seat was taken away.

As we graduates filed out, Mom stood still in the shadows by the bleachers, holding her purse tightly in front of her. She left before I could greet her.

· · • · ·

IN MY GRIEF-FILLED DAY-TO-DAY life, I hadn't thought about what would happen after college. Kate, who'd also been at my graduation, scooped me up like a melting glob of ice cream before I became a worthless, sticky puddle at the bottom of a barstool. She needed to move to Asheville, North Carolina, for a new job, but Brian had to stay in Rockford to finish a certification program before he joined her.

We drove from Galesburg to Asheville and found an apartment that she and Brian would share. I stayed for the summer, adopted her lifestyle, ate her diet of beans and rice, lifted weights at Gold's Gym, and walked everywhere possible. I was in a gentle form of detox, salvaging a health I'd never really had.

Kate and I hiked the Blue Ridge Parkway, just behind our apartment, every day. Hiking the blacktop road with a switchback, we would labor up the mountain, energized and protected by the dense forest around us. My atrophied muscles tore and grew with every step. Kate, a triathlete, was fit. I, just out of an indulgent spring term and senior party week at college, was not. Still, it felt good to be challenging my body in ways that didn't sacrifice gray matter.

On one of these hikes, we talked about our year in France when we were kids, about the hell it had been for Mom and Dad, and for us. As we sweated up the hill, I more than she, Kate said, "Did you know Dad tried to kill himself after Mom left him in France?"

I stopped in my tracks, breathing hard. I didn't know that. And it explained so much.

"No. What the hell? How did you find out?" How could I not know this? I tried and failed to imagine my quiet and often gruff, resistant-to-action dad making such a desperate move.

"Dad told me when I was a senior in high school," Kate said. "He wanted me to know, I guess. The other thing he told me is that he believes jealousy is caused by insecurity."

We resumed walking up the road. "Why do you think he told you?" I asked.

This time, Kate stopped first, her face long with memory. She said, "I was so crushed when my boyfriend broke up with me for another girl. Dad was worried about me. He thought he could teach me something about love and heartache. Maybe. I don't know."

I stared at her, still in shock. "Do you think he tried to kill himself because he thought Mom left him, left France, for another man?" A car came out of nowhere from around the switchback, just missing us.

We shuffled off the road. "Yeah. Could be. I just remember he told me both those things: about trying to kill himself and about jealousy."

"So, what happened? How'd he try to kill himself?"

"He slit his wrists the night we left him in France but then called someone for help before it was too late."

I started walking again. If I stood there, I'd cry. And I didn't cry much anymore. I couldn't believe it, but I got it. It wasn't something you told an eight-year-old. A few years later, when I was in my teens, when I had asked Mom why they didn't divorce, she'd said, "It's complicated. Maybe when you're older, you'll understand." She was right. Now I was an adult, and I understood the complication. The knowledge offered glimmers of clarity into my cloudy childhood and into Dad.

15

STILL TETHERED

"**WHAT SCHOOL IS IT?**" Mom demanded when I called to tell her I was going to be attending grad school in Chicago.

"Loyola University."

"Mmmm."

"What?" I lit a cigarette away from the phone so she wouldn't hear metal striking flint. I kept my habit from Mom, who'd quit hers when I was ten, three years before I started mine. I'd quit smoking while living with Kate a year earlier but started again after I moved back to the Midwest.

"I don't think that university is an appropriate choice. Someone must have influenced you. Negatively."

I thought by "someone," she meant Kate.

"The negative influence must have come from something or someone outside our home."

Why couldn't she just be excited for me, realize grad school was a good road map for my lost self? "What do you mean, negative influence?"

I waited for a response and heard a heavy sigh. My blood pumped. *Click.*

"Mom? Mother?"

· · • · ·

I THOUGHT LEAVING HOME meant I didn't have to see my parents or my brother if I didn't want to. Galesburg, a railroad town in the middle of the rich, black-dirt state of Illinois, had raised me as much as my family had, so I was leaving her too. I wanted to leave the pain of losing Mike and John, and I intended to put myself back together, stronger. A year after my respite summer in North Carolina with Kate, I chose Chicago over Galesburg.

I picked concrete over farmland, elevated trains over brick roads, anonymity over my small-town reputation. I set out to create a new me to replace the one formed by my family, that dirt, and that town. Leaving meant moving on, closing the door, spending time with my parents only when I initiated it. I returned to Galesburg at times to visit friends, and sometimes, when I felt guilty enough—or strong enough—my parents. I thought the physical separation would create an emotional one. I was wrong on all counts.

It was a hot summer day and my roommate was out of town, leaving me alone in our city apartment on the third story of a brownstone. The clouds, dark and heavy, offered the possibility of rain and cooler temperatures. I stripped to my bra, opened two of the third-floor sunroom windows in hopes of a breeze, and heard the clanking of an L train a block away. As sweat ran down my stomach, I sat back on the futon, opened the *Chicago Reader*, and considered quiet, air-conditioned options for a Saturday: the art institute, movie theater, Giordano's Pizza. I wilted in the city's humidity and noise, although I had spent my childhood three hours south worshipping the sun and suffering roaring locomotives.

My apartment buzzer sounded. I dragged myself off the couch, ambled to the intercom, and pressed the talk button. "Hello?"

"Hi. I'm here. Would you buzz me in?"

Mom?

I had a brief, ridiculous hope the intercom system had distorted the voice and it wasn't her. Cotton filled my lungs.

"Mom?"

"Yes, dear."

I had answered the buzzer. There was no evading, and I wasn't prepared for Mom. I never was.

The last person I expected to see in Chicago was Mom. I pressed my thumb on the button to unlock the main apartment door and then ran around the apartment hiding ashtrays.

I threw on a dry T-shirt, stopped breathing, and watched from the doorway as she sauntered toward my apartment. She wore a light headscarf knotted under her chin, lipstick, and a tan trench coat belted at her waist, a movie version of a female spy.

"What's the matter? Why are you here?" I conjured a happy-surprise face as my stomach lurched. Maybe she was running from someone recording her conversations or intercepting her telepathic messages.

She gave me the look she gave when she didn't trust someone: eyes squinty, chin to neck. "Of course you knew I was coming."

I forced a smile. I didn't want to be someone she didn't trust, but I couldn't stop myself. "No, I didn't. How could I have known?"

She slammed her keys on the hall table, pointed to her temple, and heaved a sigh. Was I the only one she thought could read her mind? She clenched her jaw. "*Of course* you knew I was coming."

Why wasn't she surprising Greg with a visit? I backed off. "How was your drive?"

"Oh. Fine. Well, not fine, but I'd rather not talk about it." Mom's eyes scanned the apartment as she spoke. From the entry hall, the small kitchen, dining room, and carpeted sunroom with the futon were all visible. I'd just moved in a month earlier, and unpacked stacks of magazines, clothes, and books neatly lined the walls, as I'd yet to determine where things should go. Besides a bed, dining set, and futon, I didn't have furniture, places to store my stuff.

I knew not to push it. Instead, I'd ease into finding out what she was doing in Chicago. "Do you want an iced tea?"

She nodded, took off her raincoat, and headed to the dining table. Mom had delusions and bizarre suspicions but could still dress for the weather, use a map, and drive 240 miles to see me.

"So, Mom, what plans do you have in Chicago?"

In a singsong voice, she said, "Have you heard of Leif Erikson?"

I poured a couple of iced teas. "Nope."

"He was the true discoverer of America, five hundred years before Christopher Columbus. A Norwegian from Iceland, I might add!"

I didn't care about Leif. Worse, I knew my day was about to be hijacked, and I'd be without a smoke for hours.

My body, all tensed up, quaked mini tremors. It had been three years since her schizophrenia diagnosis, three years since my sister masterminded a plan to get her help she didn't want, believed she didn't need. With my hands sweaty and the glasses of tea wet with condensation, one slipped from my hand and broke into shards on the dining room floor.

Ignoring the crash, she swept her arms into the air. "He was on an adventure from Norway to Greenland, and he landed in what is now Labrador, Canada!"

For some time, Mom had expressed a passionate interest in the Norwegian part of her heritage, insisting we paid far too much attention to my Russian-born dad's background. She was thrilled the true discoverer of America was, in her mind, a Scandinavian.

She waited, smiling, for my response. I froze, my chest tight. The undrunk tea and broken glass filled the space between us.

Mom pulled apart her map of Chicago and thwacked it on the table.

"I thought we'd go to Humboldt Park to see a statue of Leif Erikson. Look on my map—it's not far from here."

My mother raised her eyebrows with hope while her eyes blazed with impatience. The weight of my childhood pressed down, and I answered the only way I knew how: "Okay. Let's go see Leif."

Mom's eyes looked me up and down. "You should wear a raincoat."

I bent down and started cleaning up the spilled tea and broken glass. "I don't own one. Anyway, it's hot and not raining yet."

"Surely you own a raincoat!"

"Nope. I'd know if I did." I'd been buying my own clothes since I was sixteen and started working part-time at the mall.

I finished cleaning and grabbed my keys, and we made our way to my car parked on the street by the apartment. The clouds began to slowly release tiny droplets of rain. On our way to see Leif Erikson's statue at Humboldt Park, a place I'd never been, we stopped for food.

I parallel parked near a diner, feeling proud that it was something I did well, then ran awkwardly in the drizzle to the entrance and held the door while Mom walked up, maintaining her feminine promenade even in the rain, holding her umbrella just right to keep herself dry. Inside, she frowned as she scanned the small, dimly lit diner. Did the place not meet her standards? Or was she on guard for something sinister? We followed the host to a booth.

Mom removed her headscarf and patted her hair with her palm. "What will you order?"

My chest ached with longing as I moved the ashtray aside, picked up the menu, and tried to ignore a slight nausea. "The BLT. You?"

"I think I'll do the same. Without the bacon."

"You want a lettuce and tomato sandwich?"

This was the least strange thing she'd ordered in my presence. I should've kept quiet. I should've been thankful she didn't fire questions at the waiter about the sandwich's origins, its freshness, and then frown at his responses. Neither did she educate him on the hazards of deep-fried and fatty foods. Instead, she gazed at me as if I'd asked the world's stupidest question.

She opened a newspaper and put on her glasses. "Well, isn't this interesting?" She started to read me an advertisement for a nearby shopping market, slowly and with affectation, like it was a poem by a Nobel laureate. Then her face twisted up like a cartoon witch's. "That's an awful coincidence, don't you think?"

"What coincidence?"

She looked at me over her glasses. "No? You don't know?"

"I don't know what you're talking about." I wanted to understand what she thought was an awful coincidence. Or maybe I really didn't. I did want to know how her mind worked and what she thought of me. If she was impressed by my ability to live alone in the big city. If she was finally happy about my decision to go to graduate school. If she'd realized I was a woman now, one that she could share her delusions with. But that's just it: I wasn't ready to hear them, and she knew it. They made me uncomfortable. I didn't recognize my useless effort to please someone who could not be pleased.

She folded the paper and stuffed it in her tote. "You're too young to understand." She enunciated every syllable of every word as if she were performing it.

"How old do I have to be, Mom? I'm twenty-two years old." Still, I knew no matter what I said, she wouldn't trust me to understand. And I wouldn't. No one would.

I ate my BLT in less than ten bites. I never tasted food when I ate with Mom. My mental ripcord activated, and I floated above my body, as often happened when I was with her. She scared me. Her reality threatened mine.

She scraped the mayonnaise off her toast and, with great care and attention, ate one half of her sandwich. She folded a napkin around the other half and put it in her bag.

I wondered what she might've been like had she stayed at the hospital three years earlier, where she received a diagnosis for her illness, where she could have gotten real help. Maybe she'd have become a real mom. But she'd quit treatment, never to speak of it again. She still hadn't forgiven Kate for initiating the help. How would my day-to-day with her have been different if she'd taken it?

As we walked back to the car, I dug into my purse for my keys but came up short. I searched again, frantically, realizing I didn't have them. We stood outside my locked car in the rain, looking through the windows. My keys hung from the ignition, and the car was still running.

I'd been so thrown by Mom's surprise visit that I'd forgotten to turn off the engine and grab my keys before heading into the restaurant.

"We'll have to call a locksmith. It'll cost seventy-five dollars to have one come here and get into the car."

"It can't cost that much!" Mom was horrified by the thought. She came with me to the pay phone just inside the restaurant and waited shoulder to shoulder as I arranged for help.

I hung up. "He'll be here in about twenty minutes. Seventy-five dollars." I don't remember how I knew what a locksmith would cost.

Mom glared at me, lips tight, and grabbed my arm. "You shouldn't have said it."

"What?"

"You shouldn't have said it would cost seventy-five dollars before you called. That's how they knew what to charge you!"

I walked away from her into the rain. From the sidewalk, I looked back and watched her open her umbrella. My heart thumped because I was about to lose it. "That's *impossible*, Mom! It was just a good guess!"

She caught up with me and glowered. "You don't know what I know."

My clothes were now soaking wet. "What do you know? Maybe you could tell me. Maybe you could tell me how a locksmith five miles away heard me and decided to increase their service charge!"

I was sorry I questioned Mom as soon as I did it. Our family didn't question her delusions. We'd learned. Mostly, she'd get angry and lose further touch with reality. Yet I'd been away long enough, and my confidence, my unwillingness to just ignore the crazy, had started to bloom.

I wanted her to make sense, not say ludicrous things that weren't even debatable.

This time, my temper calmed her down. "Never mind," she said, turning toward the restaurant. "Let's just wait indoors."

· · • · ·

TWO HOURS LATER, NEAR dusk, we made it to Humboldt Park. The rain had stopped its pelting, but my shirt still clung to my body from the humidity as we walked around looking for the statue. I thought about my original plans for the day, a movie and the pizza place. I'd have ordered a deep dish.

Mom, likely 70 percent Norwegian, gazed at the statue of Leif Erikson. "The Scandinavians just don't get the credit they deserve." She motioned me, nearly 50 percent Russian and clearly an insufficient 35 percent Norwegian, over to the statue. "Let me take a picture of you in front of it. You'll want to remember this when you grow up."

Looking back now, I understand that the emotional untethering I'd imagined after moving away from my parents was a fantasy. Why I sought approval from someone I knew was incapable of providing it, I don't know. Conversely, being open to listening to her tangled view of the world wasn't something of which I was yet capable.

I finished the day as I had started it: surrendering, giving in to the illness, staying quiet and captive to the havoc it could still inflict. I stood, shoulders slumped, beneath the proud, shield-wielding Viking as Mom snapped the picture.

16

SOLITUDE GUARDIAN

A YEAR AFTER GRADUATE school, I sat in a cubicle in a skyscraper in downtown Chicago, trying to understand the concept of "grossing up" income to cover an employee's tax hit from a relocation . . . a responsibility of mine in my new human resources job. I was happy to answer the phone when it rang.

"Hello, this is Liz."

"Hi, Liz. Can you guess who this is?"

I knew who it was. I'd spent the last four years hating him because I couldn't love him. My skin prickled, and my stomach dropped. I felt faint. "What can I do for you, John?" I held the longing inside.

I had kept his voice, the voice that had blanketed me with comfort after Mike's death, tucked deep. Each time I unwrapped what had once been a healing gift, an ache spread through my chest until I wrapped up the voice again.

"I've been thinking a lot about the past. I have some regrets, and I'd like to write you a letter. Would that be okay?"

I agreed it would be okay, and I gave him my address.

In his first letter, he wrote that he'd been walking along the Mississippi River in Minneapolis, examining his past actions, ones he was proud of and ones he wasn't. He regretted how our relationship ended. He also thought about his future, and he couldn't stop thinking about me.

For the next few months, we wrote long letters, picking through the weeds of our time together in college. Love, grief, attraction, and guilt. Feelings that had come all at once, feelings with roots entangled and inseparable, feelings we'd had no words for when we were twenty-one and in a tragic situation.

The pace of exchanging words through the US Postal Service resulted in a layered understanding between us. We had time to think, write, wait, think some more, and read before writing again. I'd lost ten pounds, and the surge of hormones in my brain created an overpowering optimism—anything was possible. By the fourth month, it had been the longest high of my life. I knew we'd be spending our lives together.

We started meeting in Wisconsin on weekends, staying in bed-and-breakfasts. He proposed to me on his birthday weekend, after six weeks of long-distance dating. We were in Baraboo, having arrived late, and were just about to head to sleep in our Victorian bed. I had known it was coming, somehow, and I knew I'd say yes, but I asked him if we could go to sleep and talk about it the next day.

After lunch at a small neighborhood Italian restaurant, I told John I didn't want to have kids, or at least I needed to be certain of my own mental health before I became a mom. Inside, I was still my thirteen-year-old self, lying naked on Sherry's roof and thinking about Mom's fractured brain and its impact on me. John, similarly broken from a family history of alcoholism and mental illness, understood. I had a long trek ahead. I chose to walk with John.

· · ● · ·

MY FIRST CALL WITH the news was to Sandy-Mom. She invited us to her home, where we sat outdoors on lawn chairs on a sunny early autumn day. She poured champagne, raised her glass, and made the toast: "To Izzie and John."

I wrote to Mom and Dad to share the news. Dad wrote back, "I'm sure you're making the best decision for you. I look forward to meeting John." It was simple, and he seemed to realize he didn't have a say in the matter. Yet it was what I needed to hear, because some sort of approval was still important to me.

Dad and John had both studied literature. I asked them each for ideas for readings at our wedding ceremony. John suggested a section in *Letters to a Young Poet* by Rainer Maria Rilke, a somber section that proposed two married people should not try to be one, that although marriage was a serious undertaking, it was indeed full of possibility for each person. I was dumbfounded when Dad responded to my request by proposing the same passage:

> The point of marriage is not to create a quick commonality by tearing down all boundaries; on the contrary, a good marriage is one in which each partner appoints the other to be the guardian of his solitude, and thus they show each other the greatest possible trust. A merging of two people is an impossibility, and where it seems to exist, it is a hemming-in, a mutual consent that robs one party or both parties of their fullest freedom and development. But once the realization is accepted that even between the closest people infinite distances exist, a marvelous living side-by-side can grow up for them, if they succeed in loving the expanse between them, which gives them the possibility of always seeing each other as a whole and before an immense sky.

DAD MUST'VE REFLECTED ON his own marriage when he suggested it for our wedding. Perhaps the idea of infinite distances existing between the closest of people helped him in his union with Mom, though neither succeeded in loving the expanse between them. It wasn't a top-ten, feel-good wedding reading, not a 1 Corinthians 13:4 about love being patient and kind, but like me, neither my dad nor my fiancé was a fairy-tale romantic. Rilke was the perfect choice.

John and I vowed in our ceremony to be each other's solitude guardians, encourage each other's development, and try to always view the other against the backdrop of light and possibility. We wouldn't try to become one or ridicule each other's choices. We wouldn't follow our parents' examples; there were many places to find role models besides our childhood homes.

Keeping with Rilke, John and I chose his poem "Pathways" for the front of our wedding program. In reading the poem, we envisioned ourselves sneaking away from the popular but pointless. We'd choose quieter paths that deepened our connection to each other and to nature.

17

DISRUPTING PATTERNS

THE QUESTION STARTED COMING as I reached my early thirties and John and I had been married for five years. "When are you two having kids?"

An aberration, not having kids, and it made people uncomfortable. I knew people expected other people to want to have children.

Between my reluctance and fears and John's uncertainty, the deal was sealed—no kids. We both understood, as much as people without children can, that our biological role models would be detrimental to our parenting. I'd read enough about cycles of family dysfunction to know we'd likely repeat their mistakes, despite our best intentions.

· · • · ·

DURING THIS TIME, GREG and Dad sparked their way across the rough terrain of being father and son. Dad's expectations and Greg's behavior never did align. Dad, financially prudent, valued discriminating buying habits and a strong work ethic. Greg valued big-screen TVs, expensive stereos, and unearned income.

Dad quit drinking, without ceremony, around the time John and I married. The subsequent change in behavior was most notable in the evolution of his relationship with Greg. He gave my brother his only vehicle, even though Greg had only recently gotten his driver's license back after going years without it because of multiple DUIs.

I asked Dad when he and Mom visited, "Why did you give him your car? You don't have another!"

"I can walk to work. Greg needs it more than I do." He looked away and spoke quickly.

"What's going on, Dad? How can you trust him?"

Dad's face softened, and he looked at me. "I choose to look at the good. Only the good. I focused on fixing him most of his life, and it didn't get me anywhere."

We didn't talk about it further; I was surprised we got that far. About a year later, Greg received another DUI. As a result, the car he was driving, Dad's car, was impounded, and Greg lost his license again.

Greg and Teri, his high school sweetheart, whom I had warned in college about his cheating ways, married in time for the birth of their first child. Beautiful Alexandra, born with hydrocephalus, underwent emergency surgery to have fluid drained from her brain. But the damage had already been done. The doctors diagnosed her as legally blind with cerebral palsy. Hers would be a life of medical interventions and dependency.

Greg and I lived within twenty minutes of each other in Minnesota, and I babysat Alexandra when Greg and Teri had their second child, a healthy baby girl named Amanda. We stayed in touch while his kids were young.

· · • · ·

ONE JULY, I DECIDED to visit Mom while Dad was on a sabbatical in Russia. She seemed pleased with the idea of me coming, or at least she didn't actively try to stop me.

I was thirty-three, living in Saint Paul, and had learned in my job how to work to change dysfunctional patterns in organizations. During my visit, I decided to apply my work skills to my interactions with Mom. I'd disrupt our patterns by listening, by staying, and by accepting and not reacting, even when her words made no sense to me.

As I approached Galesburg, farmland extended to the horizon: processions of planted crops, an endless parade of green flowing prairie. The musty, dark earth and the ripening corn brought memories of muddy fields, tugging tassels, dragging on Marlboros, and longing to fit in. As I drove into town, my body churned with youthful excitement, fear, longing, and sadness. The sensations overwhelmed me, and I considered stopping at a friend's house for a drink.

The urge to follow my typical path—visiting friends for hours or days before braving my childhood home—was strong. I passed the small, old homes and boarded-up buildings outside of town, some train crossings, the four-block downtown, the town square, more train crossings, and turned onto the brick road of Broad Street to my parents' driveway. One pattern broken.

An evergreen tree Mom had planted in an awkward spot on the front lawn had grown substantially and god-awfully. It served its intended purpose, to block the view into the dining room, but its now-tattered and looming presence somehow exposed us.

As always, Mom had large books, dictionaries, and encyclopedias open everywhere on the coffee table, end tables, kitchen table, and countertops. Each one was open, covered with notes written on the pages and Post-it notes filled with cursive I couldn't read.

We engaged in our usual small talk: *How was the drive? What's the weather like in Minnesota? What's new in Galesburg?* The entire time, Mom moved around, looking anywhere but at me.

When we were finished, she motioned me into the living room. "There is something upsetting me—I want to show you."

I recoiled, then came back to the moment and my goal to stay, to listen.

"Do you see all of these books?" She was now in front of a bookcase we'd acquired after Great-Aunt Hilda and Uncle Ivan had passed away. The twelve hardcover books on the shelf were old and brown with frayed bindings.

"Yes, what about them?" I asked.

"They have all been ruined! Can't you see? Look at this!" She pointed to the bindings, which had aged over the years, her stress palpable. "Vasily did this! Honey, why would he do something that would upset me so?"

I tried to remain calm. "Why do you think Dad did this?"

"Well, who else? Who else would?"

Catching myself, I said gently, "Mom, I'm so sorry that you're upset. I would be too if I thought someone had damaged something of mine intentionally."

She turned to look at me, seeming a bit surprised. "It *is* upsetting." She needed some compassion, someone to listen. I didn't affirm or deny that Dad had done something like create little fringes on the bindings of a set of books. I listened, unruffled.

Mom revealed more of her thoughts over the weekend. Whenever she did, her thin face, worn by the years of constant torment, contorted, and her small, sunken eyes blazed. I withered under the intensity. My automatic parachute engaged, and I started to float away. *Stay*, I told myself. *Stay.*

The success of the first day with Mom gave me hope in my new approach. Over the weekend, our conversations took a different turn.

"What are your plans for having children?" she asked as we sat across from each other on their patio.

"I'm not sure, to be honest."

"Oh, you must! Having children is a joy like no other."

She sounded like she did whenever she said, "Of course I love my children very much." Like it was something she was supposed to say, not something she felt or experienced. She said it in her affected style of speech, and I initially dismissed it.

She was my frightening role model of motherhood, yet over the past few years, I had been able to acknowledge the strength of my mental health, of my rational thinking, of my resilient nature. My deep desire for clarity, for being bold in my honesty, had become a driving force of my personality after the confusion of my childhood. I had become intolerant of elephants in the room, whether with colleagues or clients at work or with groups of friends, and I called out what other people wouldn't. I vowed to not pull the shades on dysfunction, knowing that nothing would change if the truth were hidden. My courage in this area had given my tentative, shy self power and earned me respect.

My mind felt elastic and stable—able to achieve an advanced degree and success in professional work. I had a strong marriage. Why not children?

"Well," I said to Mom, present and in the moment, "I guess it's not out of the question."

2

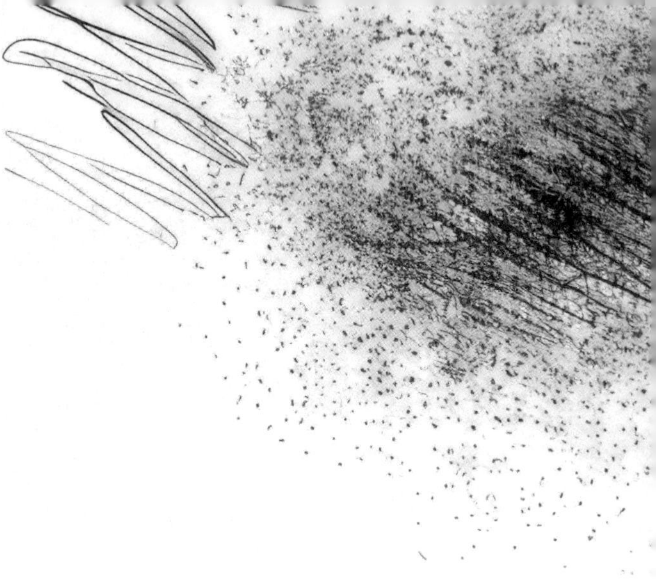

DAD'S STROKE

IN 2005, MY OLDER daughter, Katya, started calling my dad *Grandpaseely* because she couldn't pronounce *Grandpa Vasily* (va-SEE-lee) at age two. It stuck. He signed his letters and cards to our family "Love, Grandpaseely."

When my middle child, Elena, was one, she brought out my dad's giggles. She giggled at bouncing balls, at our pets, at other people laughing. She'd start giggling and look at him to be sure he was paying attention; then he'd giggle, then laugh hard, showing his large dark-yellow teeth. Then she'd start again, back and forth. When she was eight, she and Dad would each joke that the other one was "trouble." "Goodbye, Trouble!" they'd say. The last time they saw each other, she screamed it as she hung out the window of our rental car, and Dad, in his BEST GRANDPA EVER sweatshirt, waved from his front stoop and hollered it back.

I'd watch from my porch as he and Mom arrived from the Pacific Northwest, where they now lived, for visits. The moment he stepped out of his car and saw our house, Dad moved a little faster, and his smile overtook him. He worked with Mom, helped her along, but he couldn't wait. As Mom scowled at his impatience, my son would lunge toward Dad. Just in time, Dad would drop to his knee and open his arms to embrace the kids.

My brooding dad, who had preferred drinking over parenting when I was growing up, had become an exuberant grandpa to my kids, and I loved that about him. I loved him, but I didn't know him, and I didn't think he knew me, not really. We never spoke about the important things, the things that make our bodies hurt, our blood pump, our voices quiver.

In early August 2013, Dad had a stroke. Mom called Kate, who emailed me and Greg in the middle of the night. Kate saw no reason to wake us; she'd have an update on Dad's condition the next morning and we'd talk then. The medical staff at the hospital appreciated having just one contact for the family not present. I left that job to Kate, who worked in a hospital on the other side of the country and who typically took charge.

That morning I realized my dad and I might never know each other, that the opportunity might be gone. This thought-shard pierced my heart.

I dropped the kids off at climbing day camp and parked our white minivan in the adjacent lot. Sticky garbage and food crumbs from a weekend road trip littered the car. I turned off the engine, took a deep breath, put in my earbuds, and called Kate. I imagined her in the home she shared with her husband and teenage son in Crozet, Virginia. Oval face, blond bangs, green eyes sharp and alert. Her eyebrows migrating closer to each other, forming a couple of deep parallel creases above the bridge of her nose, worry lines she'd inherited from Dad. Kate focused on the call with her younger sister, me: still the baby in the family at age forty-five.

"So, Kate, what happened? What did Mom say?"

"She said Dad fell and couldn't move, so he called to her. Once she realized he needed help, she called 911."

I gazed out the van window and had a flash of Dad lying on the floor in his little room across from Mom's, in their new one-story house a half mile from the Pacific Ocean. I shuddered. I still saw Dad as I had as a kid: impenetrable, armored with PhD prestige, gruff. He'd survived the harshest of childhoods. I still wasn't too clear on the details. It was hard to imagine my Russian-born father, at age seventy-three, not being able to get up. Perhaps earlier in his life I could have imagined it, when he was still drinking a lot, but not since he'd been sober.

Dad had had this retirement house built when they moved from the Midwest back to evergreens, mountains, and ocean, back to where they had fallen in love. In my imagination, he tried to shout, but a hoarse voice broke through: "Cathy. I need help. Cathy." His clothes smelled stale and spicy from the remnants of spilled onion and mustard.

My hands tightened around the steering wheel. "Oh god, did she call right away? What if she ignored him, like she does?" I turned the minivan on for air-conditioning. "Or, what if she thought his soul was hijacked by an evil drone hovering over their house?"

"Right." On a different occasion, Kate would've laughed. "I spoke with one of his doctors. The good news is he was given tPA."

"TP what?"

"It's a drug used to dissolve clots and improve blood flow to the brain."

My friend and her daughter walked toward the climbing camp. They waved. I waved back. Most people were having a normal day. "Sounds good," I said.

"It should be; tPA improves outcomes from ischemic strokes if given within a few hours." Kate, with her health care background, knew much more about what Dad was going through. Though I had no idea what an ischemic stroke was, this seemed like the best news from the morning's ordeal.

"I'm looking into flights leaving tomorrow," she said. "I'm at my laptop now."

Kate and I often traveled together as adults, getting away for long weekends to seek fresh experiences in new cities. Big sister, little sister. Achievement-oriented, pleasure-oriented. Six years separated us, but that gap had narrowed in adulthood. This trip, and many subsequent trips, wouldn't be for fun.

"I'll need a couple of days to get things arranged for me to be gone. Have you heard from Greg?" I looked in the back seat of my van and noticed how filthy it actually was.

"No," she said. "You?"

"No. I'll call him when we hang up." An expected five-minute conversation with Greg could last an hour. Educated, persuasive, and self-medicated, Greg twisted the truth and challenged rational thinking. He'd switch from recounting his superhuman abilities and expertise to complaining about being a victim—in society, in our family, and in life. He lamented his plight, his pain, his relationship with his ex, Mom, unemployment services. He'd tell us about how he'd been the victim of this scam or that robbery, explain that he'd lost all his money or his job and how it was always someone else's fault . . . but now he needed money.

These conversations wasted Kate and me, left us hungover. He often reached out to both of us at once, and even a small delay in response would escalate his resentments. So we took turns answering.

Kate broke into my thoughts. "Dad was transferred to a larger hospital. Oh, and so you know, Mom is suspicious of the place."

"Because it's religion-based or because he's in a hospital at all? Or maybe she thinks it means Dad's fate has been decided?" I often tried to decipher Mom's strange remarks. When I was growing up, she was in and out of religion, one week dragging me to a mainstream Congregational church and the next week scowling at the idea. Her affiliation at this point was Christian Scientist, and she avoided modern medicine for her own reasons, ones she wouldn't often reveal. At seventy-three years of age, Mom never took prescription medicine. She cut multivitamins and baby aspirin in half, to save money, and took those once a day.

"Who knows?" Kate was no better at decoding Mom.

"The timing is unbelievable. Can you imagine how her mind is dealing with this coincidence?" I leaned my dripping armpit over the air-conditioning vent.

We'd visited our parents in June, just two months before Dad's stroke. Kate and I had wanted to get as much insight as we could from Mom and Dad about their end-of-life-care wishes. While both my parents were in their early seventies, it was my husband's experience with his dad that had prompted my quest. John's dad, Larry, had not had his affairs in order, and he'd suffered a sudden subcranial hemorrhage. His family had to decide how Larry should live and how long he should live, all without his input. Family members came to different conclusions, but under the law, John's stepmom, not John and his brother, got to decide.

Mom had rejected a health care directive on principle. She felt that even thinking she needed a directive would somehow manifest a situation where a directive would be necessary. In her mind, it was safer to believe she didn't need one; Dad having a stroke two months after our request for their advance decisions wouldn't add up to simple coincidence.

Kate shared more. "It's incredible. I just spoke with his lawyer; Dad filled out a health care directive, assigned me medical power of attorney, and had a will drawn up. He heard us! But he hadn't been in to sign anything yet. So it's not legal. The attorney said Dad didn't share any of this with Mom."

I knew why Dad wouldn't share this information with Mom, but the words came out anyway. "Oh my god, why the hell not?"

"He didn't want to upset her."

Still stunned that Dad had taken this step with the lawyer, I wondered if Mom was onto something—better not prepare for the worst or it'll happen. She was tricky that way, always spinning her paranoia to sound plausible.

Before we hung up, Kate said, "His appointment to sign everything, if you can believe it, was today."

I stayed in my van in the parking lot, and I called Greg. Though we lived in the same metropolitan area, I hadn't seen him in years, and it had been a month or two since we last spoke.

"Hey, Liz." He cleared his throat. "What's up?"

"Kate sent us an email last night. Sounds like you haven't seen it."

His low, slow-motion drawl sounded a bit more alert. "No, man, I'm just now rolling out of bed. Couldn't sleep." Before I could give him the terrible news, he continued, "Yeah, I hate to complain, but no one's gonna hire a felon, and before you say it, I'm not going to take just any job. I won't work at SuperAmerica."

I sighed, already impatient. "Kate's email was to let us know Dad had a stroke last night."

"Oh, for fuck's sake." I could hear in his slow, quivering voice that my words left him scattered, full of fear, but I didn't have time to empathize. I told him Kate and I had spoken and were getting on planes as soon as we could, Kate first. We'd overlap for two days, then I'd stay after she left.

"Yeah. I'll get out there too. Won't be easy, with my back. I'm low on meds. My docs are real pricks about refills. Shit. Might take me a while."

"How about you come after I do? We'll tag-team it, and that'll give you a chance to get things straight with the doctors."

"Liz. I don't even have money for our bills. Gisela pays for everything already. How am I supposed to buy a plane ticket?" He often raved about Gisela, his second, much younger wife, and her career.

"Mom will help; she'll pay for you to come."

She always paid for Greg.

· · • · ·

AFTER TALKING WITH GREG, I sat in the climbing camp parking lot, body numb. Life was happening around me, but I couldn't move.

After several minutes or an hour, I drove, my mind a mix of clarity and chaos, to a toy store to pick up a gift for my son, Elliot, to take to a birthday party—a regular errand on an irregular day. The summer sun journeyed across the sky while I moved through the thick of the day, a pace apart.

Inside the toy store, I stared through the wall of LEGO boxes. *Just pick one*, I told myself. *It doesn't matter which one—it's crazy you are here at all.* My phone buzzed. The caller ID told me it was Brian, my sister's husband. He rarely called, and my heart lifted, anticipating his warmth.

"Hi, Brian," I said with the weight of commiseration.

"Liz. Hi. I wasn't sure whether or not to call."

"Of course you can call anytime." I sidestepped away from a group of young kids screeching and pushing one another to get a better look at a LEGO set I was standing in front of.

"It's just that Kate . . . Well, I'm worried about Kate."

"What's wrong? I just talked with her. We put together a plan to fly out to Seattle." What could have happened in the last hour?

"Yeah. She has a real tough time dealing with your mom." I could tell by his soft, slow voice that whatever was going on was not urgent, but it was important. He had a goal for this call, but I didn't know what it was.

"I know. I do too." This felt weird; he knew Mom was hard on all of us. I, of all people, knew how hard she was on Kate. Didn't I?

"Okay. Well, Kate gets *really* anxious, and your dad, well, he won't be available, so she'll have even more interactions with your mom . . ." He paused like I should guess his intentions.

"She isn't alone in this." My heart raced, and the words came out fast and curt.

"You know what? I hesitated to call, and I realize now I shouldn't have. I'm sorry. I'll let you go." His pace was quicker, and his tone had changed.

"Okay. Bye." I was happy to hang up. This is how communications always went in my family. Brian knew. Hang up or walk away before it gets real.

What did he want from me? I paced through the aisles and grabbed the LEGO set the kids in the store were excited about.

I'd been defensive, scared him off, and now I wouldn't find out why he'd called. In the checkout line, I sent Brian a text declaring again that Kate wouldn't be alone in the situation, that I'd step up as I had with the advance directives, that my stress level with Mom impacted my life too, that I understood. He replied that I had misinterpreted his understanding of things, that he took the blame for that and he shouldn't have called. He was sorry.

My gut twisted. It *was* different for Kate. As the oldest, she had long suffered in the most dangerous of positions: in between my parents. Back when she was just thirteen, in France, he had confided in her, promised her he'd quit drinking, and begged her to stay with him. Kate and Dad had a strong relationship, they knew each other, and Dad would not be there to be a buffer for her with Mom, who'd never been kind to Kate. Being with our parents now was going to be extra challenging for us both, but I hadn't fully considered, and Brian likely had, what we were on the verge of.

18

APHASIA

THE RENTAL CAR SMELLED of stale cigarettes and upholstery cleaner, so I rolled down the driver's side window. The warm sun on my arm felt good, calmed my nerves. A glorious yet daunting Mount Rainier loomed over the highway. Mount Rainier and the Space Needle. When I was a kid, when we'd visit from our small, flat midwestern town, it was big deal to be able to see those grand landmarks, surreal in Seattle's rainy climate—now you see them, now you don't.

I squeezed the steering wheel, wishing I could go faster. Highway construction around Tacoma was doubling my drive time from the airport to Olympia, and all I wanted was to be at Dad's bedside, seeing for myself how he was doing.

I called Kate to let her know I was on my way. She was alone with our double whammy parental units: Dad incapacitated, with his health care directive and will unsigned, and Mom, mentally unfit but holding tight to her rights as Dad's medical power of attorney.

"I'll be there in about an hour. How're things?"

"Not good. I guess you should know before you get here." Kate paused, and I swallowed hard. "The medicine they gave Dad to dissolve the blood clot ended up causing a secondary brain bleed. It's rare, but it happens, often when they don't give the drug within three hours after the stroke."

The placement of yellow cones narrowed the road, and I had to concentrate to not drive over them. "They must have gotten the timing from Mom! She thinks the fatty pizza he ate that night caused his stroke! There's no way she was tracking time."

Kate sighed heavily. "In addition to his right-side paralysis, Dad's second bleed caused global aphasia. It means he can't speak or understand speech, and he may not know language at all anymore." Her voice cracked. "He may not have his memories. He may not know us. It may or may not be temporary."

Temporary, please, temporary. It's gotta be.

"We have to see what happens when the blood engorging his brain has time to drain."

I leaned forward and gripped the wheel tighter. I blinked hard to keep my focus on the cones.

· · • · ·

I ARRIVED AT THE hospital, jumped out of my smelly rental car, and tried to quickly stretch the four-hour flight and two-hour drive through congested traffic out of my legs. I arched my lower back and breathed in tangy pine and sweet cinnamon. If Dad had to be sick somewhere, at least it was in Olympia, a nature-rich spot in which to recover. A town on the edge of the pristine waters of the Puget Sound, with views of the Olympic Mountains, surrounded by a force of vibrant greens: Douglas fir, western hemlock, and western red cedar.

I glanced from the gigantic trees above to the freshly cut shrubbery that surrounded the front of the hospital and a sign that read "Healing

Garden." I followed the path through the garden toward the cold sheen of the polished floors inside the hospital. Why was Dad in the barren hospital when clearly the healing elements were outside?

Inside, I picked up my pace through the antiseptic smells, through the stroke unit, and halted before Dad's door. Hesitating, I inhaled deeply. I realized how unready I was. Would he know me?

Exhaling, I stepped into the room and saw Dad in his bed, propped up a bit and covered to his chest in white sheets. He was awake, and his color seemed good. Relieved, I rushed to him and put my hand, jittery, in his, heavy. He moved his head to face me, but his expression didn't change. His favorite sport, soccer, was on television, and he didn't seem to recognize that either.

Mom sat upright in a chair in the corner. Her walker was against the wall, and her tote bag was hanging on it. Her tote bag carried unfinished meals, small notebooks filled with undecipherable writing, extra clothes, no less than ten tattered checkbooks held together by a taut rubber band, a key chain with twenty keys to places she no longer had access to, and her wallet. At eighty-five pounds, her body appeared tiny, like I was looking at her through the wrong end of a telescope; a miniature doll in an oversize dollhouse. Her face scrunched up like it does before she makes an accusation. I'd been in the room thirty seconds, and I already felt woozy and unfocused.

Kate leaned against the windowsill next to Mom. Her shoulders reached for her ears. She smiled at me with relief, and I felt it too seeing her.

Quick hugs, a tight one for Kate. I leaned down for Mom's. She sat spine straight, as always, eyes sunken and clothes hanging off her bones.

"You look nice, dear. Doesn't she, Katie? What a beautiful skirt and blouse you have on!"

I bristled and looked toward the window. I saw my reflection: a cheerful flowered skirt, a mint-green sleeveless blouse. I liked the outfit I had picked out for travel, and maybe I'd picked it out for her because she'd always been critical of my appearance. But it didn't matter what I was wearing, and I realized I hated that she'd focused on it, that her focus had always been on my outside, never my inside, never *me*.

Dad. The lines between his eyes were gone; his face was placid, unexpressive. I walked back to his bedside, and he looked at me, his hazel, almond-shaped eyes meeting mine. I held his arm, but there were no words, no voice. Silence.

In his eyes, I read shame. Or disappointment. Did he know where he was? Did he think he could've prevented this? Maybe he was angry with himself for moving Mom away from us kids, the ones who would be left to care for her. Perhaps I read in his eyes his awareness of the tragic irony in having a stroke on the day he was to sign his health care directive and will.

Tubes fed his veins, and bruising colored his thin skin surrounding the points of puncture. His black hair, combed to the side and back as usual, showed the rectangular plane of his wide, shiny forehead. His receding hairline, his mustache—everything the same but somehow different on his new impassive face. I wanted him to knead his mustache with his fingers, back and forth, as he did when deep in thought.

Then, aha! I realized something huge: he was not wearing his glasses—the glasses he only took off for brief moments to rub his tired eyes. Those moments created a gulf between Dad and his world, a disconnect I felt every time. Afterward, when he'd put the glasses back on, I'd feel a rush of excitement watching his eyes reconnect to his world. When he saw me, it'd appear that he did know me, and not just the outside of me, or a photograph he'd taken and liked because it was a version of the me he wanted me to be.

A nurse entered the room to change Dad's catheter bag.

"Please, Nurse," I said, "where are his glasses? He needs them to see!" My heart rose as if this small change would somehow fix everything, bring him back to pre-stroke Dad.

The nurse picked up the glasses on the desk beside his bed and placed them on his face. "These are the ones that came with him in the ambulance."

I waited for Dad's reappearance, but his gaze, his searching, confused eyes, endured. I deflated. Where was the man who quoted Tolstoy, translated Russian to French, loved foreign films, fishing, and watching hours of soccer? Where was the man who for thirty years had led college students on tours of the Soviet Union and Russia during the Cold War, opening a misunderstood and closed culture to our small-town community? Where were the round belly and thick skin that deflected Mom's daggers? Tears formed in my gut and came out my eyes.

Dad's right side was still, and his eyes moved slowly around the room. When he bent his left knee and his penis appeared through a gap in the gown, I jerked my head toward the windows, toward the mountains, evergreens, and mist on the other side of the glass. The room had a spectacular view of the Olympic Mountains. It was a natural world of lush beauty where I wished my dad could be. I'd be with him. We'd walk the woods, like we had at Green Oaks on a good day, Dad with his pole and me tagging along with the tackle box, looking for the lucky fishing spot. He'd say, "You'll hook your own worm this time, right, butterball?"

Mom's voice jolted me. "Why, he doesn't need potassium! Take that IV off!" she said to the nurse, who was monitoring Dad's fluids. She grabbed the rail on his hospital bed to get closer to the action. Decisions were being carried out without her say.

The nurse smiled and nodded at Mom but went ahead with changing Dad's IV fluid bag, saying nothing.

Mom softened and tilted her face. "He just needs some vitamin C and honey. Can you put *that* through your IV?" she asked. Before the nurse could answer, Mom went on to offer her knowledge of the benefits of honey versus all that "high-tech stuff" the hospital provided. Her fear of "high tech" had started in my childhood. "The walls have ears," she had warned us; there were "high-tech" listening devices everywhere. I would run my hands along the textured wallpaper in our hallway and think, *Where are the miniature microphones?*

The nurse continued her work while she listened to Mom. When Mom stopped talking, the nurse spoke to Dad loudly. "I'm going to readjust your pillow to make you more comfortable. How's that? Much better, right?"

Mom scowled. I scowled too, but inside. *He has global aphasia—he's not deaf! He's got a PhD and speaks several languages—he's not dumb!*

And yet, he *was* dumb. Now that I was with him, I understood it better. His brain was swollen, and we would have to wait until the blood drained before learning what his life would be like. In the meantime, all his language and comprehension—verbal and written, auditory and visual—were gone. Dad didn't know what we were saying, he didn't know what our gestures meant, and he couldn't form words or speak. The linguist and his language, lost.

· · • · ·

A NURSE WHO HAD worked the night shift gave us an update on Dad. "He got some good rest, I think. He wasn't as restless as he has been."

As the nurse relayed the daily information on his vitals, if Mom's eyes narrowed and her face twisted up, that indicated the incoming communications had been corrupted. If she smiled and nodded softly, approvingly, I could relax.

Kate and I followed the nurse out of the room as we'd been doing after every update. "Excuse us," I said.

"Do you have a minute?" Kate asked. "We want to let you know a little bit more about our mom."

The nurse cooed, "Oh, your mom is so cute, so sweet!"

I cringed. After forty years of unnerving people with her wild accusations and wacky behavior, Mom was now seen as a harmless elderly woman, albeit with a plate of dementia and a side of paranoia. But my mother wasn't harmless to Kate and me. She was an avalanche ready to bury us with rocks of grief, anxiety, and guilt.

"Oh. Yes. Thank you. She can be sweet." In my shock, I searched for more to say to the nurse about Mom.

Kate piped in. "We're sorry she can seem rude . . . questioning the nurses. She doesn't believe in medicine and technology. She's suspicious of both."

The young nurse kept her smile and nodded before walking away.

Kate, frowning, motioned me down the hall to a quieter spot. She clasped her hands protectively in front of her chest, and I sensed something big. "I think we should tell the nurses and doctors that Mom has untreated schizophrenia." She waited for my reaction. I nodded. "Not just to help them understand her behavior; we've got to find a way to take decisions about Dad's life and health away from her."

Our mom has schizophrenia.

My heart had thumped and my hands tingled the few times I'd shared this information. Each time I confided in someone, to help them understand Mom or me, I felt guilt, as if I'd exposed her, since she'd never acknowledged the illness. I didn't know about anosognosia yet, and for decades, she seemed to try to keep up the appearance of normality. It's also true that my pride made it difficult for me to suffer the shame, the stigma. Kate felt the same and for a long time as an adult didn't talk openly about Mom's schizophrenia and about Dad's alcoholism.

After keeping her condition secret our whole lives, I believed that when the time came to use those words, they'd have the power I'd given them all those years. While in the hospital advocating for our dad, I thought if we used the medical term for her brain illness, the staff would understand she couldn't possibly make decisions for our dad.

"I totally agree," I told Kate. "We need to tell someone here who can help us."

Kate dropped her shoulders a bit and lowered her arms, and we walked back into Dad's room. Mom's face was tight, the corners of her mouth weighted.

"Let's get some lunch, Mom," Kate offered.

Mom's face eased. "Yes, let's do that. Afterward, Katie—or Liz, for that matter—neither of you have much to do here. Can one of you take me to get a pedicure?"

We were trying to understand our dad's chances for recovery, for mobility, speech, and quality of life, and she was worried about her toenails. I looked at Kate, who was looking at me with her eyes wide.

· · • · ·

FOR A FEW DAYS, Kate and I kept trying to be in the hospital room with Dad to get an updated prognosis when the doctors did their rounds. In my estimation, the doctors were in Dad's room about ten seconds a day. Somehow, we'd mostly missed them.

Dad seemed worse, not better. He had attempted to speak the day Kate arrived and seemed to recognize her. Now, he no longer tried to talk, he appeared sleepy or confused, and it was clear he didn't know who we were.

The doctors we happened to catch skirted the topic. "It's still possible for the blood to drain," one neurologist said. "We need to wait and see how things progress in the coming days," said the internist.

Nurse Regina was on the day shift with Dad during the first week. She was a tall woman with dark hair she wore pulled back in a sleek ponytail. We listened as she gave instructions to the other nurses about Dad's care, his medicines, his nutrition. She was calm, efficient, and direct. We relied on her. We'd confided in Regina about Mom's illness, even Dad's thwarted end-of-life wishes. She'd been sympathetic, but like everyone else, she could do nothing to help.

Regina glanced sideways at Kate after the most recent doctor again left us with no information on Dad's prognosis. "You've been asking about your dad's condition. I thought you might want to see this." She pulled up Dad's latest brain scan on the computer in the room. While Regina was silent, we were able to see Dad's brain full of blood. It was hard to see any part of it not impacted, but the left hemisphere was especially dark, as if colored with a black Sharpie.

The image was a lot worse than we'd expected, and I swallowed a lump when I saw it. Yet for the sake of our mental health in the moment, we held on to the possibility of recovery. We sat in his room desperate for answers, for a glimpse of Dad. Each day, we waited to hear from the cardiologist, then the neurologist. The physical therapist came. Could Dad sit up on his own? He couldn't. We watched the occupational therapist work with him. We were excited to see whether he could hold a spoon. He could, but he had no idea what to do with it.

It had been too long since his stroke. There was no more waiting for blood to drain, to see if there were parts of him, parts that made him Dad, still there. He was Dad—there, but not there. The chance to understand him and for him to know me had perished before I'd considered the possibility that there was a deadline.

As we tried to fall asleep in our room that night, Kate rolled over on her bed to face mine. "I'm not going to be able to sleep again tonight. All I can think about is Dad's future and how he'll be alive, but only on machines."

"I'm sorry. It's an awful thought. And just what he didn't want."

"I feel responsible," Kate said, and I imagined her blood pumping and pulsing with oldest-child duty. "The only other time I've felt something similar is when we left Dad alone in France."

That's the first time I realized she carried the weight of that horror even though she had been just fourteen years old at the time.

"I'm sorry." I didn't know what else to say.

· · ● · ·

KATE AND I TOOK turns pushing Mom in her wheelchair for meals in the cafeteria. She hated it, the wheelchair and being wheeled, but she agreed; it would be too far for her to walk to the cafeteria each time we needed to go. We wheeled her up and down so she could see what food was available, waited as she made her choices and changed her mind and made special requests. I worried about us holding up the line for doctors, nurses, and patients' families.

On one of these trips, as the three of us walked through a wide hallway near a gift shop, Mom suddenly stretched out her arm and waved it around. "Look at this crowd of people wearing plaid!"

I glanced around and saw three people, none of whom was wearing plaid.

"It's an odd choice and insulting!"

I decided to ignore the hallucination and ask a much more pressing question. "What? Plaid? Why is it insulting?"

With her cheeks sucked in and lips firm, she said, "If you don't know, I don't think I should tell you."

My normal response would be to let it go, to pretend she hadn't said something crazy. If I did that, maybe it would leave both our minds. But I wanted to know what the hell plaid ever did wrong, and for some reason, I expected a reasonable answer.

Instead of letting it go, I said, "If you tell me, then maybe I can agree—it's insulting." I felt focused, strong. A greater power, my focus on Dad, dismissed my brain's usual escape protocol.

"Well, honey!" She sighed, and her small, underfed body made a dramatic movement of exhaling, her chest sinking, pushing her shoulders forward. With her delicate, bony hands aiding in her speech, she said, "Your father planted all those Scotch broom plants in our yard without even *asking* me! I can't stand them . . . yellow everywhere! Good Lord. I was planning on hiring someone to come dig them all up, just to show him, and now all these people are wearing plaid."

Kate stepped into the elevator, held the door, then flipped her head back toward me, swallowing a laugh, eyebrows arched high. I wheeled Mom onto the elevator, where there was a man standing in the corner wearing a red, green, and white plaid shirt. Mom scrunched up her face and said, "See there. That's the shirt that offends."

He didn't respond. Maybe he didn't hear—oh, I hoped he didn't hear—or maybe he too had activated a survival parachute: ignore, pretend you don't hear the crazy talk. I white-knuckled the handles to her wheelchair and remembered to breathe.

We got off the elevator, left the offensive-plaid-shirted man behind us, then stopped for a moment. Mom focused on me, her face serious with an extra bit of white exposed around her small and round hazel eyes. Despite her age and angst, one could still see the beauty in her face, her high cheekbones, wide mouth, long neck. Her reality oppressed her, mocked her, told her people were trying to hurt her for ridiculous reasons. Yet, her indignation about the pattern plaid had caught me off guard.

After making sure I was looking at her, she said, "Can you take me for that pedicure now? It's Monday, and businesses with bisexual connections are closed on Mondays."

19

FORGIVING

A HOSPICE NURSE FRIEND told me the three gifts you could give a dying person were to say, "I love you," "I forgive you," and "I will be okay." I wanted to do this for Dad, but we weren't that kind of family. I'd never heard "I love you" from Dad. With Mom, I'd heard, "I love my children very much. Of course." When I was growing up, during the establishment of our family culture, we had fought, and we'd mumbled. Verbal communication happened when necessary—whereabouts, dinnertime, acceptable temperature on the thermostat, what to watch on TV, laundry, money, a bit of politics, and foreign culture. Nonverbal expressions were rampant. Crossed arms, averted eyes, walking away, sneers, eye rolls, slammed doors, sighs. Expressions of apology and offers of forgiveness, love? No.

· · • · ·

I LIKED BEING ALONE with Dad in the hospital, talking to him, though I didn't think he could understand. I could say things I wouldn't if he were responding. I held his thick hand, stroked its leathery skin, my thumb traveling the contours of his veins. "I remember the good things too," I said out loud. "I love you, Dad, and I'm going to be okay." I rubbed his arm and tried to say, *I forgive you*, but I couldn't. A gift denied.

For a week, Kate and I cared for our dad, now helpless like a newborn. We combed his slick hair and took turns feeding him. The nurses would run out of time and patience, and he wasn't getting enough calories as a result. We had nothing but time.

The first time I fed him—small spoonfuls of his pureed diet of peas and sweet potatoes—I offered him the spoon too fast for his swallowing muscles to keep up. He started to gag.

Mom wanted to help with the feeding, but it was a standing job and physically would be too hard for her. She gave orders from her chair, waving her hands for emphasis: "Feed him the other one. Oh, this is silly. He can certainly feed himself. Slow down, honey! Though he should be used to it. Vasily has always eaten far too fast and too much!"

I put smaller amounts on the spoon and slowed down. After several minutes of slow eating, he got tired and looked away, just like my kids did as babies to announce they were done. I waited, ready with another spoonful hanging in the air. After getting confirmation from Kate that she thought he was done too, I wiped his mouth, cleaned his mustache. He looked at me, his eyes locked on mine, but I couldn't find him in his eyes like I wanted to.

· · • · ·

I WOKE EARLY THE next day to sneak in some alone time with Dad before going back to meet Kate and Mom at our hotel next to the hospital. Today, maybe I could give him the third gift.

I walked into his room and found Mom sitting in the corner chair. It was 6:30 a.m. How long had she been there? She must've used her walker to make the long walk, or perhaps she got a shuttle ride. I felt guilty, as if caught in a deception by not following our routine.

After motioning me over, she whispered in a serious tone, "Your father wants to be alone with me in his hospital bed to have sex. What do you think about that?"

I looked at Dad, asleep and with global aphasia, and I looked at Mom, so tiny in her chair with her walker leaning against it. I said, "I don't think it's a good idea. He isn't in any condition for that activity, Mom, and how would you know he even wanted it?"

Sex and sexuality were private, unspoken matters in our family. The Puritan was alive and well in Mom. My birds-and-bees talk, like any other subsequent talks of importance, came in the form of Ann Landers columns left on my dresser. This is how Mom encouraged me toward abstinence and communicated to me about the methods of birth control, a year after I had started taking the pill.

Prim and prudish, she'd taught us to keep our privates private. She was obsessive about it. No one shared a bathroom. In our house of privacy, we locked the bathroom door and we closed our bedroom doors. I didn't see her naked, and she didn't expect us to see one another naked.

Greg ridiculed her message of chastity and self-restraint. He'd laughed when he told me that he'd opened his *Hustler* magazine to the centerfold, where the woman spread her legs open to reveal all—the clitoris, the labia, the vagina—and positioned it on his bed for Mom to find. I felt bad for Mom, whom I saw as virtuous and prudish, coming across this magazine on her son's bed.

Did she now see me as someone old enough to talk about sex with?

Mom adjusted her bony butt on the chair and pressed out her chest, her head forward a bit, her chin up. "Oh, I know by the way he was moving his hand. A woman knows these things."

I imagined one of his involuntary movements, which the stroke had caused. He tended to kick his good knee out to the side and move his sheets around, like he was trying to get comfortable, not request sexual favors.

"Okay, Mom, but maybe the hospital isn't a good place for that. It's not private here."

"Oh, right, yes." She nodded with what seemed like relief. "It's not a good idea."

Were they still having sex? She didn't like him. In all my life, I'd never thought she liked him. He was the giant sponge that soaked up her verbal assaults, her accusations. The major offender, according to Mom—the person out to harm her the most—had always been Dad.

"Why must you one-up me all the time, Vasily?" she'd demand as he pulled out his camera to take photos of his grandchildren. "He's always doing this, and it is awful, just awful!" Her face would scrunch up, her gestures violent. She'd slam her hand on the table and whip out her own camera. "I can take pictures too, see?" And we'd all begin our eggshell walks. Her bad moods tended to turn to psychosis.

Mom's accusations against Dad included his taking her things and giving them to other people; causing the fruit she wanted to eat to over-ripen; moving a table to make it more difficult for her to get around; having sex with his brother's widow and the widow using pillows beneath her bottom for more pleasure; causing the bindings of old books to fray to upset her; buying electronics and high-tech items that read her thoughts or caused her pain. Yet now that he was debilitated, she considered making love to him.

Mom and I sat in Dad's room, silent. Still reeling from her question, I tried changing the subject. "So, Mom, when did you and Dad first meet? When he first came to the United States?"

Mom perked up. "I sat across the room from him in French class. He was fluent in the language, and I was impressed. I did not ask for it . . ." She lowered her head, but the corners of her mouth moved back to a smile to light her eyes. "I was assigned the job of interviewing Vasily for the school paper."

I sat back. I had never heard this story. "Was this when you two started dating?"

"Not quite, but he was very persistent," she said. "He called every day and would walk to my house, hoping to see me." She softened and blushed. I wished Dad could hear her. When was the last time he'd heard her speak with such fondness for him?

"Was it love at first sight?" I moved to lean against the window ledge closer to her chair.

"I think he liked the way I looked," she said matter-of-factly.

"He fell in love with the idea of you, then?" I was enjoying this conversation.

Her eyes ignited. "Yes, that's right," she replied, like I'd hit on something she hadn't realized. "And we came from such different backgrounds."

"What did your parents think of you dating Dad, someone from a different background?"

"I don't think your Grandpa Howard cared for it, though he didn't know how smart Vasily was." She sat even more upright; her eyes brightened. "One day at school, in the hallway, your dad had his report card sticking out of his back pocket." Mom paused and placed her hand to her backside. "I reached behind him and snatched it out. I was surprised to see it had all A's!" She opened her eyes wide and smiled. In her face, now appearing decades younger, I could imagine a teenage girl, flirting with Dad, not unlike how I'd flirted with boys in high school. It was risky behavior: seducing the smart and mysterious foreigner, the boy her father wouldn't approve of.

Mom, gazing at Dad and still smiling, closed her mouth, and I watched her chest move up and then down as she slowly exhaled.

· · • · ·

DAD'S CONDITION REMAINED UNCHANGED, and he didn't seem to be a candidate for rehabilitation or sex, yet no doctor would tell

Mom or us that. Maybe they were still waiting for a miracle, or maybe no one with authority was willing to discuss how a small stroke had ended this way. My guess is the doctors didn't know how to talk with us about the death of Dad's essence, his soul.

One day, after hearing our frustration about not getting a prognosis from the doctors, Regina motioned Kate and me into the hallway, away from Mom and other hospital staff. "I want to let you know what kind of life your dad will have," she said. "This is what you're wondering, isn't it?" Her voice was soft, infused with purpose and warmth.

"Yes!" Kate said.

I nodded. I kept nodding and taking deeper breaths as she spoke.

"He won't walk again. He'll be paralyzed on one side. He'll need help eating, and he'll need personal nursing care. He won't be able to read, write, or speak." She took a large, deep breath, then continued. "Your dad's weak heart and his diabetes will require constant skilled medical care. The physical and occupational therapists here said there was nothing they could do. I'm so sorry."

Kate rubbed her knuckles. We thanked Regina for not pulling her punches. After she walked away, we held each other.

Even though it hurt, I was prepared to hear the truth. For days, the knowledge of Dad's condition had pressed against my rib cage, up to my heart, and down into my gut. Now that it was out in the open, I was relieved. Relieved someone had finally had the sense to acknowledge what we already knew.

· · • · ·

I TOO NOW WORRIED about Dad suffering for years in a condition he'd wanted to avoid. I hadn't been eating much of anything; my clothes were loose. We couldn't get a copy of his unsigned legal documents from the attorney, and Mom resisted the notion that Dad had ever had those documents drawn up.

Kate and I had spoken those words that I had deemed to be so powerful. *Our mom has schizophrenia.* We told a few nurses and a couple of doctors. But it didn't change anything. She was still legally the person in charge of Dad's health care and end-of-life decisions.

We had texted and phoned updates to Greg daily about Dad: how he seemed, details about his vitals, whether his atrial fibrillation was under control, whether he could eat or not, and how Mom was doing. For our morale and his, we tried to be optimistic and focus on the positive in our updates.

He'd asked about Dad's pain medication, which was Dilaudid. When he heard the name and dosage, he laughed. "That's less potent than what I take on a normal day!" But underneath his usual loping drawl was an added quiver.

Kate and I decided we needed to let Greg know what Regina had told us, and we needed to involve him in the code status discussion—DNR/DNI, meaning Do Not Resuscitate/Do Not Intubate—before he arrived. We sat on a bed in our hotel room looking at Kate's iPhone, talking with Greg using the speaker setting.

"Hey, guys, how's it going? Greg asked.

"Not good. Dad's in bad shape," I said.

"What the hell? What happened?" he asked.

I realized that in trying to stay optimistic for our own mental health, we hadn't been completely honest with him.

Kate continued, "We learned from a nurse today that he isn't going to recover, and he isn't a candidate for rehabilitation. He'll need to go to a nursing home." Her worry lines were deep, and her voice cracked.

"Jesus Christ. No fucking way. I need to be there. What do the doctors say?"

"They won't discuss prognosis," I said. "The nurse showed us Dad's recent brain scan. She believes the damage is permanent."

"And if he has a life-or-death event with his heart or diabetes, they'll do everything to treat him, even though his quality of life would be worse after," Kate continued.

"Won't the doctors just do what he said he wanted? He wanted DNR!"

"Nope. Mom is Dad's legal medical power of attorney. She isn't going to address his code status. She won't even talk about it."

"I can talk to her. She listens to me, for some reason. We can't have someone who has one foot in Cuckoosville making life-or-death decisions for Dad."

We agreed he should try talking with Mom. We had nothing to lose, though we didn't think he could get through to her either.

· · • · ·

MORNING MIST RIMMED THE dark forest outside of Dad's hospital room. Mom, Kate, and I assumed our regular spots: Kate and I along the window ledge near Dad and Mom in the corner chair. Beeps from the equipment monitoring Dad's vitals had become background noise I couldn't decipher. Each time its sound changed, my heart would jump, and I'd look at Dad, who remained still and unchanged.

Kate examined Dad's pureed breakfast menu and picked up the phone to place the order. Mom's facial expressions changed like she was interacting with someone, but she said nothing.

Loud, quick staccato beeps suddenly blared from the monitoring equipment, and I whipped my head toward Dad; he seemed unaltered. I looked up again, and a flood of medical specialists flowed into the room.

"What's going on?" Kate asked Regina.

Regina spoke quickly. "Code blue. It's your dad's heart. The cardiologist is on his way. You guys should step out of the room."

Mom resisted. I grabbed her canvas tote bag to hurry her along, and she yanked it back, waited a moment, then got up and inched out of the room now filled with new nurses, specialists, and equipment.

As we walked Mom to a seating area down the hall, someone asked, "What's the patient's code status?"

Dad's heart had experienced extended periods of ventricular tachycardia that could lead to cardiac arrest, so once he was stabilized, they moved him to the coronary intensive care unit. The doctors had been managing his atrial fibrillation since he arrived, but this development was new, and he needed additional care and monitoring.

When it was okay for us to see him, we found Dad asleep in an enormous bed like a king's throne in the center of a spacious corner room, windows on either side. The room offered an unexpected respite from the cramped activity of the stroke unit. Now on the first floor, I could almost reach out and touch the thriving green plants in the hospital gardens.

While the word *intensive* might suggest vigorous activity, the atmosphere was serene, and the nurses slow and deliberate. The calm spread to Dad, who slept with less agitation. I wanted him to stay in the peaceful setting, closer to nature. I wasn't advocating for vitamin C and honey like Mom, but I wanted the outdoors and its healing elements closer to Dad.

· · • · ·

I GRIPPED A PIECE of paper with talking points for a difficult conversation I planned to have with Mom over lunch. Kate had helped me write them, as Dad's almost heart attack had made us realize the stakes had gotten higher. We needed to get his end-of-life-care wishes documented, and fast, before additional emergency medical care left him more medically dependent. Just saying Mom had schizophrenia wasn't enough for the hospital to let us make the decisions. We thought we'd make one strong attempt to have her provide the code status Dad wanted, before looking into legal action.

Kate was happy to let me go it alone, and we hoped Mom wouldn't feel ganged up on if it were just one of us. Kate wasn't sleeping. Her anxiety seemed on par with mine, but at least I was getting sleep. She told me she'd been lying awake worrying about Dad and how she felt she had a job to do and couldn't do it because of Mom. I wanted to take some of the burden off. I thought of Brian's call, of how Kate had a stronger reaction to Mom's instability, and of how Brian might have been wanting me to step up and do this exact kind of thing.

When I first saw Mom that morning at the hotel, it was clear she hadn't slept. "Let's get some breakfast, Mom. You look tired."

She shot me a glare. Her skin was ashen, pants twisted at the waist. "I'm fine. You don't look so good yourself," she snarled. Mornings were usually her best times.

I pushed her wheelchair a bit faster.

"We should take your father home today," Mom said.

What she was suggesting was unreasonable, impossible, but I couldn't say so. Not when she seemed on edge.

Kate and I knew who to call at the hospital if Mom had a psychotic break. It wasn't hard to imagine; we'd seen it before. She'd lose grasp of her pretending skills and she'd start loud-talking nonsense; her bizarre, illogical connections and accusations would spill out, and she'd be unable to catch her breath. She'd get louder and angrier as anyone listening could only show disbelief. She would hurl cruel criticisms. She'd become the person we were careful to keep hidden. When she was psychotic, we were the ones to crack.

Mom had rested and seemed better by lunchtime, which brought me relief. She no longer talked of taking Dad home that day. I wheeled her through the hospital cafeteria lines as she made her choices with great care. At the cash register, Mom reached from her wheelchair with money in her hand. The ginger-haired cashier with dream catcher earrings asked, "Are you together?"

Mom looked up and back at me but didn't answer.

"No, separate," I said. I meant: *I don't want to be together with her. Nor does she ever seem to want to be together with me.*

I wheeled her to a sunlit table away from the noise. I folded and moved her wheelchair out of the way of foot traffic, made repeated trips to get water, utensils, and napkins, and we settled down to eat.

She wiggled and tried to get comfortable in her chair, and I took a deep breath. "Mom, Kate and I wrote down some things we need to talk about."

"All right," she said as she used her white plastic fork to push aside the cheese from her salad. She looked at her food with a skepticism meant for me.

"The doctors are asking again about Dad's code status. They need to know if we want them to intubate, revive, put in a feeding tube—these sorts of things—you know, if he gets worse. If he has an emergency."

"Mmmm." She looked at me earnestly.

"So, you know Dad had a health care directive, right?"

"No, I don't believe he did."

"Yeah, he did! He used an attorney in Ocean Shores. Just last month. He didn't want doctors to lengthen his time in a situation like this if he wasn't headed to a better quality of life."

She furrowed her eyes, shifted her head back on her neck, looked at me like I was crazy talking, like I was seven years old, telling her some outlandish story I'd heard on the playground.

I pleaded, "Don't you think you should let the doctors know this?"

"Whatever I say, it won't work. They'll use it as an excuse."

"An excuse? For what?" I leaned across the table so she'd know whatever she said, no one else would hear.

"To change how they are treating him, of course."

"But that's just it—they won't. They'll continue to treat him as they are now. If, though, he has a massive heart attack, as an example, then what you decide matters."

She had moved all the cheese to one side of her plate and was now using her plastic knife to wipe the mayonnaise off her sandwich. She was underweight yet worried about eating too much fat. "Mmmm. If I tell them a code status or just think it, one way or another, they'll change their care. And they want him gone. You must know this."

"What do you mean? It's their job to try to make people better."

"Maybe when you're older you'll understand." She sighed, opened her mouth to speak, snapped it shut again, and went back to scraping the bread. "I happen to know," she continued, "they'll take what I say or even if I just think it . . . Don't you see?" She pointed dramatically at her head. "They'll use it to change their care and as an excuse."

"Excuse? For what?" I knew what she meant, and I couldn't believe it.

"Well." She stopped fiddling with her food and kept her eyes on mine. "Killing him."

I left her gaze as soon as I could and stared at my food that I wouldn't eat. I'd lost five pounds in the week I'd been there.

After a protracted silence, I said, "Mom, if the doctors can read your mind, maybe you want to reconsider giving the responsibility of medical power of attorney to Kate or to me? I know this is a heavy burden for you, and I'm pretty certain they don't have access to our minds."

Her eyes opened wider, and she lifted her chin and declared, "No! I'm the wife!"

She knew what we were trying to do. She might have had bizarre battles in her mind, but that didn't mean she wasn't quick-witted and tuned in to our sad, impossible situation.

The attorney Dad had worked with in Ocean Shores was semiretired, which meant semi-to-not-available. After he told Kate about the documents Dad had planned to sign the day of his stroke, he never returned her calls. Finally, we stopped calling him, understanding the unsigned documents were worthless. What other recourse did we have?

Kate and I focused on building relationships with the new doctors and nurses in the CICU, as we had with Regina and the stroke unit staff. When Mom was not around, we explained to these folks, who were rational, that our mother was not.

We asked the doctor who'd cared for Dad his first night there if she could help us. We wanted to take medical power of attorney from Mom and give it to Kate, and we were seeking legal ways to do this since Mom was unwilling. The doctor confirmed it would be nearly impossible. No doctor had treated her for her brain health in the past twenty-five years, and due to privacy laws, those records wouldn't be available to us; given the length of time that had passed, they might not even exist.

Mom was able to care for herself and, by law, make her own decisions. With no psychiatrist to say she wasn't competent to perform the duties of medical power of attorney, we were on our own to make this case. We could go to court, to petition for guardianship of Dad, have Mom evaluated against her will to determine competence, and cause a family storm that would take time, money, and emotional tolls on all of us. Attorneys told us the odds were not in our favor, not if Mom could keep it together for an evaluation. We knew our mother would fight; she was strong-willed and determined. She could charm an evaluator and a judge, and we would lose—on all fronts.

Dad's heart stabilized, and he was moved back to his tiny stroke unit room, where people whirled in and out. I spoon-fed him pureed meat. He seemed uncomfortable, uninterested in eating. He looked into my eyes, then away.

20

CODE STATUS

BEFORE THE MEETING WHERE we thought we'd be able to influence Dad's fate, Kate felt the weight of the world on her shoulders, so she and I split our first-ever Xanax.

In the conference room, facing our mother and then turning to Kate and me, the doctor said, "Your husband's—your father's—situation is serious and complicated. It's important that you know how your decision on code status would impact our treatment of him in a number of catastrophic situations, or emergency codes, typically related to cardiopulmonary arrest."

"Please explain," I said. I wanted the doctor to be specific so Mom understood. "What would you do if he had a heart attack or if he couldn't breathe? How would you respond? And what kind of life would he have after?"

The doctor explained how they would change their care if Mom decided the code status was to be DNR-CCA: Do Not Resuscitate–Comfort Care Arrest. "Under this status, we would continue to treat your husband full code, meaning we would do anything possible to keep him alive unless he cardiac arrests. With his heart issues, this is a strong possibility. If he cardiac arrests, we stop all medical treatment and provide comfort care. If you choose DNR-CC, comfort care only, we would ensure he's comfortable by treating fevers, giving pain medications, et cetera, but we wouldn't resuscitate him in an emergency situation."

Mom raised her eyebrows and said, "Well . . . I happen to believe you should stop giving him potassium. And a little vitamin C might help."

Kate and I shared a glance. She had the look of exasperation I felt.

The doctor looked at Mom, paused, then continued. "A separate DNI—Do Not Intubate—is required with DNR-CC; without it, a breathing tube will be inserted in his throat or lungs to help him breathe if he can't breathe on his own."

Struggling myself to follow all the situations, the codes, the ramifications, I knew Mom might be lost. Yet I continued our unreasonable quest for her to get it, to understand as we understood. "What would his life be like after an intervention like one of these?" I repeated. Kate shifted to the edge of her seat.

The doctor sighed and said, "Your father's quality of life would be worse than it is even now."

Mom looked up. I hoped she was tracking this, that she understood what she had to do. "I think it was the frozen pizza he ate that evening," she said. "Do you think that fatty pizza caused all this?"

Why did I think this might work?

"Mom, there's no way—" Kate caught herself. It was useless.

The doctor looked at Mom closely. "No, I don't. I'll go now, and you three can discuss this further. This is hard. I'm sorry."

After she left, we sat in silence for a moment before Kate said, "Let's get some fresh air, spend some time outside."

We wheeled Mom to the garden, to a bench in the shade near a stone fountain. Her face morphed; she seemed pained. I hadn't seen her cry since I was a child, but I thought she might.

"I think I should talk with Carol," she said. Maybe she did know what was at stake. She didn't trust Kate or me, and she wanted to talk with her sister. Mom was closer to Carol than she was anyone. It was strange Carol had not visited since Dad's stroke. She lived just two hours away. What was keeping her from coming? As far as we knew, she was in good health, still doing Norwegian dancing, socializing, and otherwise enjoying life in retirement. Kate dialed Carol's number and gave Mom her phone.

Kate and I walked around the garden to give Mom privacy, and I allowed myself to get hopeful again. We watched Mom, trying to interpret what Carol was saying on the other end.

Mom finally nodded before reaching her hand out to us with the phone. She smiled. "Carol said, 'Vasily will be just fine! He is a strong man, a man of good stock!'"

Mom decided to not give a specific code status, which meant the medical staff would treat Dad as full code. The doctors would do everything they could to save his life, though his mind and half his body were useless.

Kate was livid. I took Mom to the cafeteria while Kate tried to reach our cousins, Carol's children, to see if they might be able to better inform Carol of our situation. She left a message with one about how Carol had done exactly what we needed her not to do: give Mom unrealistic hope grounded in fantasy.

Carol, no one yet knew—though her daughters were beginning to suspect—had Alzheimer's.

That evening, Kate and I walked Mom to her room early and drove to a liquor store to purchase our dinner of capped wine, no corkscrew needed, and junk food. Back in our room, I propped up the pillows and sat back against the wooden headboard and stretched out my legs. Kate twisted open an inexpensive bottle of pinot gris, filled two plastic hotel cups to the brim, and then sat against the other headboard.

"I can't imagine doing any of this without you, my favorite *seestor*," she said.

"I was thinking the same thing. What am I going to do when you leave"—I took a gulp of wine—"and Greg shows up?"

"Luckily, you leave the day after he arrives." She smiled slyly. We had arranged it that way.

"Right." I smiled back.

We drank and filled up. I opened some veggie chips and Dove dark chocolates. My appetite was coming back.

Kate unwrapped a chocolate and read the wrapper. "'You're exactly where you're supposed to be.'"

I chomped on a chip. "Maybe open another one?"

Kate grabbed another chocolate and unwrapped it. "It says, 'Buy both.'" She looked at me, and we rolled our eyes and chuckled at the same time because we never bought both.

Kate's smile turned flat. "You know what really makes me mad? Mom kept us from Dad. She made it impossible for us to have a relationship with him. We'd be having a good conversation and she'd walk in the room, and that'd be it. She'd accuse him of something, and he'd clam up or walk out. Even recently. When I found out Dad was letting Mom read his emails because she didn't trust him, I didn't feel I could be honest in my messages anymore. I had to edit them down to nothing."

I let a chocolate melt on my tongue. "Imagine how life would be different if she could have been a real mom to us."

Kate smoothed out the Dove foil wrapper until it gleamed. "I can't imagine," she said.

"Yeah. Me neither."

"If she could be a real mom, maybe we wouldn't have such a hard time picking out Mother's Day cards." She used quote signs with her hands. "'To the Best Mom on Mother's Day: There's so much to admire about how you do motherhood.' It takes so long to find the one that just says, 'Wishing you a nice day.'"

I laughed. "True! Though, because we have the parents we do, I have this enormous range of what I find acceptable. Seriously, people can pretty much break every social rule and I'm cool with it. I like that about me, and whether that ends up being good or bad, I think I owe it to Mom."

Kate nodded and smiled, then frowned. "Having Mom as a mom has never seemed harder than now, trying to take care of Dad."

I swallowed my last bit of wine.

Kate would leave the next day, and Greg would arrive the day after that. I shuddered thinking about Greg taking over after I left.

On the morning Kate was to head home, she visited Dad in his stroke unit room. Afterward, she grabbed her luggage, and we sat on a bench in the dew-covered healing garden and waited for the shuttle to take her to the airport.

"How'd he seem?" I asked.

"He's sleeping too much. He doesn't have energy to eat. The nurse mentioned a feeding tube." She sighed. "I don't want to have to decide, or for Mom to have to decide, when to remove it." She arched her lower back and then moved her head side to side to stretch her neck.

I swallowed hard. "I'll spend lots of time feeding him. I'll go as slow as he needs me to." I thought of being there without Kate and then waiting for Greg to come so I could leave too. What condition would he be in when he arrived, if he arrived at all?

The shuttle pulled up, and I wanted to cry, but I couldn't. Maybe I'd used up all my tears as a child. Kate and I hugged each other tighter and longer than normal before she boarded.

· · • · ·

ONE OF THE FEW times I'd seen Greg in the previous ten years was at a gathering at my house when Mom and Dad were in town. Looking for my toddler, I'd wandered into the front room and found Greg leaning back in a chair, a baseball cap brim low on his brow.

Glaring at me with cold blue eyes, he said, "Nice house."

Our cousin Gina had once told me it was Greg's jealousy of me and Kate—of our lasting marriages, healthy children, professional jobs, and comfortable homes—that drove his anger. That didn't make sense to me, though, because whatever drove his anger had been at the wheel a long time. I'd suffered Greg's hostility toward me since we were kids. Before marriage, children, and a house of my own.

The event that caused me to build my highest boundaries with Greg had happened while Mom and Dad prepared for their move from Illinois to Washington State five years earlier, after Dad retired from teaching. Mom needed to make decisions about her belongings, but being attached to every piece of paper, candle, and book she owned made the downsizing process near impossible. A baby grand piano she had inherited from Aunt Hilda and Uncle Ivan was on her list of items to part with.

"Honey, do you think your children will play the piano?" she had asked me over the phone.

"Yeah. I think they will. We'll get them lessons."

"I'd like you to have the piano, then. I gave Greg the one you grew up with ten years ago, and, well, since he lives in an apartment now, you should have the piano."

"Thanks, Mom! That's wonderful." I thought it would be great to have the piano. It was old, resistant to tuning, and not worth the moving bill, but it was from my favorite relatives, Great-Aunt Hilda and Uncle Ivan.

A couple of weeks later, while I sat on my daughter's bed as we read bedtime stories, I answered my phone. Bypassing the small talk that she was most comfortable with on the phone, Mom started speaking as soon as I said hello.

"Dear, I've changed my mind. I'm giving the piano to Greg."

She paused, and I managed to swallow my reaction and stay quiet.

"Well, dear, he *was* the piano player, after all," she said, baiting me. She expected a fight. I felt my throat thicken and my blood pump.

"He could play the piano so well. And even though he doesn't have much room for this piano and his kids are grown, I do think it should go to him."

I said nothing. Anger surged through my body, and I couldn't think straight. Why had I believed her? I knew better than to accept anything from Mom. I made a vow to not ever ask her for money or anything she valued. It never turned out well; she'd change her mind or ask for gifted items to be returned, or in some way hold it over me. I also knew better than to yell or tell her what I was thinking. Anger triggered her schizophrenia, or at least her expression of it.

My daughter, looking at the picture book, glanced up at me, concerned. She'd noticed the change in my energy, and I think Mom did too.

"And you could always just buy your own, for heaven's sake. You have the means." Her tone was accusatory. How dare I make a decent living!

With my face hot and jaw tight, I managed to say, "You're right, Mom. We can budget that into our spending next year. Give the piano to Greg." And I hung up.

I woke the next morning to an email Greg had sent in the middle of the night. He threatened to come to my house with a baseball bat, ready to hurt me and my family if I upset *his* mother again over something like a piano. He called me a spoiled bitch. I forwarded the message to Dad and to Kate, letting them know I would no longer initiate communications with Greg, no longer be the sister who hosted family visits, and no longer pretend I had a relationship with my brother.

· · • · ·

I WAS WAITING FOR Greg in Dad's hospital room when my phone rang.

"Liz, it's Greg. Uh. Yeah. I'm here. At the hotel."

"Okay, I'm in Dad's room. Are you coming over?"

"Naw, man. I can't. Maybe later. Can you come down here?"

I met Greg outside. He stood, cigarette in one hand, his other in his coat pocket, searching into me with desperate eyes. He swayed a bit, his upper body leaning forward, hips back. His intent stare begged me to tell him that, on second thought, maybe he should just go home.

We walked back to his room at the hotel, the cigarette smoke lingering on his clothes. He still walked with swagger but without the confidence of his youth. His face was weighted with age, and his eyes appeared smaller than I remembered, his nose larger. His thin blond hair had receded to showcase the classic, substantial Fiedorow forehead. Though he'd looked nothing like Dad as a kid, he seemed to be transforming into him now.

In his room, a line of prescription bottles stretched a foot and a half along the console table across from the bed. I thought of the little toy soldiers he played with when we were kids. He'd lined them up the same way. Dependent on medications for chronic back pain and anxiety, he had delayed his trip to ensure he'd have a full month's supply at the ready. With the crackdown on pharmaceutical narcotics, he must have had great determination to procure this reserve.

Still swaying, he grabbed a red plastic tumbler and filled it with bourbon. "You want one?" He took extra time to deliver each word, enhancing his rural Illinois drawl.

The walls closed in around me, and the pill bottles and tumbler were all I could see. "Greg, I'm thinking maybe those drugs and that drink don't go together."

"Geez, Liz. It's hardly anything given the situation here. And when did you get on a high horse and become a teetotaler?" He laughed like I would laugh with him.

As much as I wanted to, I couldn't tell him to go home. I needed him here so I could catch a plane, see my family, and check in with my clients. My freelance work allowed flexibility, but I couldn't ignore my life indefinitely.

Greg took a final swig from his tumbler and stared at me, standing with my arms crossed, waiting for him. "Fine. Let's go. Fuck me, man. This is surreal."

· · • · ·

IN DAD'S ROOM, GREG hugged Mom, who beamed when she saw him. Her initial reaction when seeing him was always one of adoration and happiness, even though his trouble with the law, his inability to keep a job, and his constant requests for money, her hot button, had started to wear on her. She'd never let on to Kate or me, but to hear Greg tell it, she often "tore him a new one" whenever he phoned to ask for money, telling him to just accept any job and work his way up from there. What was wrong with that? she wanted to know. Then she'd write him another large check.

Greg went to Dad's bedside, caressed him, and held on to him like he might never let go. Dad looked at him, the same look he'd given me, but watching his eyes inspect Greg's reminded me of their adult relationship. Despite Greg's behavior, they had forgiven each other. Their adult relationship was complicated but strong, and I had forgotten that. I stepped into the hallway and finally cried.

Greg rushed out of the room and hurried toward the elevators without looking in my direction. I waited until he boarded the elevator before wiping my eyes and heading to Dad's bedside.

In the spot Greg had left, I stood and clung to Dad's arm, not wanting to step away from his warm body. My hands traveled down his forearm from his elbow—his skin soft, pale, and thin—and moved toward his stocky fingers and yellow nails. They looked as they always had, his ring finger swallowing his wedding ring. I found my own fingers had wrapped themselves around his wrist. I thought of him trying to cut himself there after Mom had left him in France. There was no evidence of violence. I placed my index and middle fingers on his radial artery, just under the base of his meaty thumb, and counted the beats of his struggling, romantic heart, still pumping life through his forever altered body.

I thought of the three gifts my friend had told me we should give our dying loved ones: *I love you. I will be okay. I forgive you.* I still hadn't given him the third gift. Had I forgiven him for drinking his way through my formative years, for ignoring my development? Was he responsible for Mom's mental breakdown, the trigger in France that had ignited her illness? Could he have done more afterward?

Forgiveness. How do you know if you've forgiven someone when the damage is so deep and lasting? Is love forgiveness? Had his focus on being a good grandparent and on being a good husband to Mom, albeit too late, allowed me to forgive? If so, I had forgiven him, because I loved him and I wasn't sure what my world, my kids' worlds, would be without him. His grandparenting of my children brought me profound joy and appreciation, yet I'll forever ache from his daily decision, when I was a kid, to drink and not to nurture.

I held his wrist, my eyes burned, as I realized gifts are as much for the giver as the receiver.

"I forgive you," I said softly.

· · • · ·

I WENT BACK TO my room and packed my bag, feeling like I was preparing to jump off a moving train. Mom and Greg together added up to something more disturbing than the sum of two maimed souls. As soon as I left, Greg would ask Mom for money, and Mom, as Greg often described it, would emasculate him with negative comments about his lack of employment. Dad would be secondary to their illnesses.

I trembled as I left the hospital, much like I had when I'd arrived. A train horn blared in my head. The peace I'd achieved by living far from my childhood home, finding my own values, enjoying a healthy family of my own, broke apart. My nerves bounced and rattled under my skin.

I called Kate from the airport while walking to my gate. "I'm afraid to get on this plane. Greg is in no condition to take over for me."

"Really, is he that bad?"

I told her about Greg and his pills and booze and his inability to stay in the room with Dad. Meanwhile, people rushed by on either side of me with their rolling luggage.

"I have to get home, but can I leave Mom and Dad in his hands?" I stopped in front of my gate area.

"You can and you should. It'll be fine. I'll be in touch with the hospital, and we'll both be in touch with Greg multiple times a day. It's his turn to be with Mom."

"You're right." I plopped myself into an empty seat. "Thanks, *seestor*. Miss you."

"Miss you too."

On the airplane, I glanced out my window seat, watched the temporary clouds below, and focused on the permanence of the mountains in the distance.

21

PALLIATIVELY

A GROUP OF SPECIFICALLY trained doctors, nurses, and other specialists known as a *palliative care team* intervened on behalf of Dad just a couple of days after Kate and I left Greg in charge. Where were they, I wondered, when we were at the hospital stressing about Dad's care and Mom's state of mind?

One team member, a psych nurse named Becky, asked to help our family. She had spent time with Greg and Mom before calling Kate. She thought her psychology expertise would help.

Kate and Becky agreed on two goals: getting Kate medical power of attorney and then getting Mom to understand that comfort care was the best route for Dad. Kate could arrange this herself if she had medical power of attorney, but she'd want us to all agree with the comfort care approach. Becky said she could help with both goals.

There was a conference call set up with Becky. While hopeful, I kept my expectations in check.

"What does Vasily enjoy doing? What are some of his hobbies?" Becky asked.

"He always liked fishing, and he was swimming at the community center up until several months ago," Greg said.

"He enjoys a good foreign language film," Mom said.

"He likes to walk by the ocean and take pictures to send to his grandkids," Kate offered.

"You know he'll no longer be able to take part in these activities, right?" said Becky. "Can you tell me if you think he'd want to be fed by a feeding tube, if necessary, to live?"

There was agreement: he wouldn't.

"Cathy, it's a difficult burden you've been carrying alone. Would you consider letting your daughter Kate, who I understand works in a hospital, take over as medical power of attorney? She could make these medical decisions, keeping your husband's quality of life in mind."

After forty minutes of gentle nudging by Becky, Mom—exhausted, outnumbered, and perhaps confused—said, "All right. Yes, I can do that." And she signed the paperwork. It was an amazing, huge obstacle overcome for us and for her. A big part of our mom must have finally wanted to be rid of the load she couldn't mentally carry.

Kate and I barely acknowledged the breakthrough, as it meant darker times ahead. Though we'd fought for the right to make Dad's wishes known since the minute we arrived, it was difficult for Kate to change his code status once she had the authority. It was indeed a burden.

She arranged for an old high school friend of Mom's, Maxine—the friend Mom had not seen for decades but who had kindly driven Mom to Olympia the night of Dad's stroke—to call and share her story of having had to make the same decisions for her incapacitated husband. Kate had learned about the story when she called Maxine to thank her for driving Mom. After talking with Maxine, Mom agreed with us to not prolong Dad's life if he wasn't going to get any better. Kate changed Dad's status to comfort care, and the hospital staff transferred him to a gentler, more peaceful setting: a nursing facility closer to their home in Ocean Shores. We had no idea how long he would hold on—weeks, months, or years.

· · • · ·

GREG STAYED AT MOM'S house while Dad was in the nursing home. It seemed to work out at first. Greg said he was more available, pointing to his unemployment status and the fact that he had no dependents living with him. We heard from him several times a day via texts and phone calls.

"Everything okay, Greg? How's Dad? Mom?" Kate asked in one of our three-way calls.

"Depends on your definition of *okay*. Been working on Dad's car. I shouldn't be doing the work, with my back, and I'm running out of pain meds."

"Maybe you shouldn't push it?" I said.

"I had to do something. It's crazy-making here. Mom makes me give her receipts when I go to the store to get food for *her*. She hasn't paid me back. I've spent thousands of dollars here already."

Though the idea that he had spent thousands of dollars he didn't have was ludicrous, I also knew stress and grief had drained them both of their functional reserves. I said, "You should take it easy. I'm sure she'll pay you back."

"You guys don't get it. *Take it easy?* I'm out of money. I've been here a month now! Well, Gisela did put five hundred dollars in my account. But that's all I have."

"Greg, you've only been there twelve days," Kate pointed out.

"What? I've been in this fucking mess for four weeks. What are you talking about?"

"Are you serious?" I had overestimated his grasp of reality.

"Greg, I ordered your plane tickets; I know the date you arrived," Kate said before backing off.

Kate and I spoke after we hung up with Greg.

"Do we really need him there?" Kate asked.

"I had hoped he'd be there a month, helping. But he's focused on money and drugs."

"Let's figure out how to help get him home," Kate said.

22

WOODS

IT WAS THE END of August, and my husband, my kids, and I had stuffed the car with "necessities" and left for our annual week at Camp du Nord, a family camp in northern Minnesota that reserved cabins by lottery eight months in advance. We sang silly songs memorized in prior years as I thought of Dad and worried. Would he die while I was at camp? Should I be on an airplane to see him instead?

At his bedside a week earlier, I had talked to him and massaged his arms. I wasn't sure he knew who I was. I interpreted the look in his eyes, how he positioned his head, his restlessness. We all did: Kate, Greg, Mom, and I. We wanted to believe he knew who we were. We wanted to believe the noise he made was a laugh and that, yes, that was a twinkle in his eye; it meant he recognized us. But I was already grieving the loss.

Our third full day at camp arrived, and John and our six-year-old son, Elliot, and I sat at the trading post playing games. The girls were at our friends' cabin. I left John and Elliot and walked through an aspen-and-birch-lined trail, admiring the white, peeling bark and delicate, pale-green leaves flittering in the wind. Then, watching my feet to avoid tree roots and rocks, I passed wintergreen, bunchberries, and wildflowers. The trail rounded by Wally's Woodshed, one of the places where campers picked up wood for their fires, and I arrived at our rustic cabin on the lake to make some calls.

Unplugged staff and camper converts frowned when they saw people on their phones at camp. My legitimate excuse for bad camp behavior didn't help, as I couldn't tell everyone who gave me the stink eye that my dad was in the hospital, having had a stroke, and my sister and I were hard at work trying to control our wild card brother, the only one of us now with our mom. So I hid in the shelter of our cabin site. About ten steps diagonally from the cabin toward the largest birch, I could kneel in a bed of old man's beard lichen and get the necessary bars on my phone to check my messages.

Crouched down with pine needles poking through my hiking sandals, I turned my phone on, waited for it to find a cell tower, and held a low-profile squat in the woods. There was a text and a phone message from Kate. Both said the same thing: "Dad passed away one hour ago. Peacefully."

A primal noise, a combination of a groan and a sigh originating at my core, rushed out of my mouth like a sudden gust of wind. Relieved and thankful, I felt my biggest burden, a burden I shared with my sister—the possibility that Dad would have to live in a way that he had made clear he didn't want—fade with my breath into the woods.

Lightened by an initial wave of relief, I wandered back down the path to my family, my body separate from my head, which was trying to connect to the reality of the news. A hollow space widened in my chest, not from the lifted burden but from the finality of the loss. I fell against a boulder and collapsed into myself. For some reason, I thought of the photo of Mom and Dad on their wedding day, of how radiant they both had looked on the cusp of a bright future. She had been his hope following his childhood of sorrow and devastation.

Back at the trading post, John sat at a table playing a board game with a friend. Elliot sat on John's leg like a bird perched on a branch.

I whispered in John's ear, "Grandpaseely died."

Elliot, with the hearing and reaction time of an owl, opened his eyes wide and said, "Grandpaseely died?"

I'd had it in mind to tell the kids later, in the evening, when we could all be together to talk about it. I walked away. I couldn't look at his round face, his sun-bleached hair, his big brown eyes. My nose tingled, and fluid filled my eyes.

Since Dad's stroke, I had tossed and turned, unable to sleep, imagining what he endured in his inability to communicate in any way, unable to say if he was hurting or hungry. Though he was now designated comfort care only, I had been scared he'd languish in the nursing home, in global aphasia and diapers, for months or years.

I thought back on Dad in his antiseptic hospital room with the magnificent mountains and forest just outside his window. I remembered wondering, as I fed him and combed his hair, why I had never asked him the questions that pursued me. What was his childhood like in Russia and Germany during World War II? Why did he stay with Mom? The severity of Dad's stroke meant I would never ask him these questions. Nor would I ask him why he drank, how he quit drinking, what he thought of being a father and grandfather. Most important, why had he not pushed Mom to get help? He'd left us all prisoners to her illness, arresting our development, denying us a healthy parent.

I'd sent digital images of the kids to Dad over the years that he had printed in extreme sizes. He wallpapered his house with photos of Katya playing the piano, of Elliot holding the antique-looking toy truck Dad had sent, and of Elena in her pink cowboy boots and gymnastics leotard.

He sent my children postcard pictures of the animals in his backyard in Ocean Shores: photos of deer, a raccoon family, and birds pecking in the bird feeder, our Christmas present to him one year.

In our home, he'd held our kids when they were babies, laughing as they tugged on his mustache. When they were older, he knelt on one knee, his belly front and center, while the kids smothered him with hugs. He laughed like I'd never seen him laugh before. Experiencing the laughter, the joy between my dad and my kids, had healed a few of the open wounds left from my childhood.

That evening in our rustic cabin, the five of us gathered on the uncomfortable log furniture and talked about Grandpaseely dying and about death. Elena plopped on my lap. John held Elliot, and Katya sat between us.

John squeezed Elliot. "I'm going to miss Grandpaseely a lot. This sweatshirt." John pulled at the frayed collar of the shirt he was wearing. "Grandpaseely gave this to me twelve years ago. I know you guys tease me because the shirt is so old and tattered, but I might never get rid of it now. It reminds me of Grandpaseely's kindness and thriftiness."

"Yeah. Grandpa wore his shirts until they fell apart too." My nose started to tingle, and I tried to smile.

Elena put her smooth, fleshy cheek against mine. "I don't have any grandpas anymore."

Katya tilted her head. "I'm going to miss his bear hugs and the postcards of the animals in his backyard."

I was going to miss my dad's enthusiasm for anything my kids did and for simply being who they were. He loved them with a love I only felt the edges of as a child.

We decided we'd speak of him often, to have him live on in that way, and then we had a family hug.

23

MEMORIAL

WHEN MY GRANDPARENTS DIED, our family didn't fly to attend the funerals or grieve with relatives. My childhood family ritual for dealing with death or suffering went like this: when someone died, we ignored the event and left the grievers to their grief. If we were grieving, we did it silently with no expectation of sympathy. We didn't attend funerals or services, nor did we send cards or flowers, bake muffins, or cook meals for those going through a rough time. I didn't know people even did some of those things until I left home.

Once, as a teenager alone in the house, I received a call meant for Mom. I picked up the receiver from the kitchen-wall-mounted telephone. Nervously, I tried straightening the coiled and tangled cord as I learned that Mom's old friend, the beautiful and kind Frenchwoman who'd moved away from Galesburg many years before, had died of cancer. Marcelene. Tall and lean Marcelene, sophisticated yet warm, who'd spoken French with a joyful throatiness in her voice. I passed along the news but felt helpless as my parents did nothing to support Marcelene's family, to acknowledge her passing and the pain that her husband and daughters, once my friends, were feeling.

My parents' "management" of their disorders upstaged grief and expressions of sympathy. They had nothing left for anyone else.

Greg buckled fast under the downpour of Dad's death and Mom's demons. He was staying with Mom and complained to Kate and me daily about how much he was spending, how his drugs had been stolen, how Mom distrusted him, and how his family must miss him. His troubles diverted our attention from Mom. Under the labor and stress of making decisions with Greg, Kate arranged schedules so he would fly home a day before we arrived.

Through conference calling, Kate and I contacted Mom after Dad passed to let her know we'd be coming soon.

"Mom. I'm so sorry. How are you?" I said.

"We're going to miss him so much," Kate said.

"Oh, it's just awful," Mom replied. "I'm not sure how I am. Not good. It's like he was always here." Her voice was quiet, worried.

"Of course. You and Dad were together for over fifty years," I said.

"I don't want to talk about it on the phone." Her nose was stuffy; she'd been crying.

We stayed on the phone for a minute in silence until Kate cleared her throat. "We can help. He didn't have his will signed, so you'll have to go through the probate process to be sure assets in his name are transferred to you. I can help with that."

"No! I'm his wife. I most certainly can do that."

"But, Mom, it can be a complicated process with lots of paperwork," Kate implored.

"I don't believe so," Mom said. "Carol told me once the probate process was a breeze."

After the call, Kate and I dialed each other to debrief.

"I'm not going out there if she won't let me help, and she clearly can't do this on her own," Kate said, grieving and furious.

Despite what I knew about her, I was still yearning for a nurturing mom. "I don't know why I expected it, but she never acknowledged that we lost our dad," I said.

"She can't possibly do this on her own. Do we let her fail first?"

"Let's give her a chance to think about it and call her later."

After we hung up, I started researching the probate process.

In our next call with Mom, we discussed the idea of a memorial service for Dad. As with the probate process, she insisted she be the one who planned the service. In her mind, she was the one who was grieving, and she wanted to plan the service with Aunt Carol, whom we still didn't know had Alzheimer's and was failing fast.

Kate, Greg, and I realized we didn't have it in us to try to pull off a service for Dad with Mom in charge and Carol involved. We postponed planning the service, and Mom never mentioned it again. In the meantime, we announced his death through obituaries and via Knox College. Knox helped by giving us the email list they had of Russian majors from the years Dad had taught. They also published a piece on Dad in their newsletter and annual report.

The letters and emails filled our boxes, mostly from former students and graduates but also from Knox staff. The messages were consistent in how they described Dad and how he had impacted them during the years he drank away my childhood.

> *I'm sorry to read of Dr. Fiedorow's passing. Dr. Fiedorow's personal stories . . . helped me to understand the Soviet Union as well as WWII. His easy style helped me to grow in many ways . . . He had a tremendous impact on my life . . . he became like a family member to me . . . If it weren't for his classes, I don't know where I'd be today . . . His encouragement, humor, and insights . . . his commitment to human rights made Vasily a memorable teacher . . . I'm a better human being for having had the benefit of his wisdom . . . He was one of my favorite Knox people, so*

kind, friendly, and generous—a bighearted person who cared deeply . . . any time you ran into him, he brightened your day.

In the end, none of us, including Mom or Carol, took the lead to make it happen. A year later, I gave up on the idea. There never was a service for Dad. That's the way he would have wanted it.

24

THE FRIDGE

IT HAD BEEN JUST a week since Dad died and three weeks since our time at the hospital. Mom's suspicions, the code status dilemma, and the revolving door of nurses, neurologists, and cardiologists were just weeks behind us but already seemed like distant memories.

Though frustrated with Mom's refusal to let her help with probate, Kate decided to come with me to be with Mom after Dad's death, and to try to help anyway. With no legal right to take over her affairs, we settled on getting her whatever resources she needed to be safe and healthy: in-home care, a house cleaner, a medical alert system in case she fell, and a meal service.

We knew she wouldn't be open to having strangers in her home. Still, we researched options, set up meetings, planned and rehearsed, and did our best to convince Mom in a way that didn't look like we were trying to convince her. She refused all services, one by one, during our visit. Sometimes, she'd reluctantly agree, only to change her mind after we'd made arrangements.

By law, she was in charge of herself.

No matter what effort or anxiety we put into it, the result was the same. Not coercible, she insisted on her competence. When we asked lawyers about taking over her affairs, we got the same answer as when we'd asked about taking medical power of attorney for Dad away without her consent: if she could hold it together for a judge, we'd lose. It's nearly impossible to have someone's individual rights taken away. That's the way it should be; it just left us in a tough spot. Mom's illness never escalated to the point where she was dangerous, which is great, but were left with no options.

Kate and I tried to focus on the positives of her living alone as we walked to the ocean for a break while staying at Mom's house. The wind off the water lashed our faces.

"If Mom can make it on her own," Kate said, "even though it might not look like what we want for her, maybe that's the best option? She values her independence more. Her bar for safety, food, and hygiene is much lower now."

I zipped up my jacket as we fast-walked. "Yeah, and who are we to say how she should live? If the law says she's in charge of herself, then shouldn't we just accept it? We can't pick her up and put her in an assisted-living home anyway." I said this knowing the other side of the argument was equally compelling. My gut and the rest of society, outside of the law, told me we needed to do something; we needed to get her someplace safe. We just had no idea how to do that.

Maybe Kate heard the doubt in my voice. She said, "Being with other humans in a senior facility might make her psychotic. She doesn't do well with a lot of stimulation."

"Ugh. You're right. Then would she just stay in her room? What if they forced her to take medication when her whole life she has refused it? Is that a good thing or a bad thing?"

"And what if we got her to a senior facility and she upset enough people that they kicked her out? What then? Would she live with one of us?"

Mom needed probate papers, called *letters of administration*, to get to Dad's assets. She resisted using a lawyer until she found she couldn't argue her way to Dad's money at the banks. They wouldn't accept a death certificate to close his accounts or put them in her name, as she'd assumed they should. "Of course they will!" she'd said. "Why wouldn't they? I'm his wife!"

A few days into our visit, Kate and I helped Mom out of the car at the lawyer's office. I looked at the small, quaint building that had been transformed into professional office space. The building was a bright spot in the fishing port and timber town of Aberdeen, thirty minutes from Mom's house.

After we sent Greg all the information about Mom's meeting, he'd said he expected to be involved in every decision made. We planned for him to attend via telephone.

The probate attorney, a tall, bald, and commanding older man named Jack, introduced himself to Mom with an outstretched hand. "I'm so sorry for your loss," he said.

Mom, smiling at the male attention, held one hand on her walker and accepted his handshake with the other. "Thank you," she said.

We sat at a round table, Jack to the left of Mom, Kate and I across from her, and the conference phone with Greg on the line in the middle.

Jack explained the probate process to Mom in his pithy, casual manner. "I'll take care of the paperwork you'll need to act as personal representative, or trustee, to your husband's estate. I'll draw up the letters of administration. With these letters and your husband's death certificate, you can contact the institutions where he has assets and have them put in your name. This includes the title to your house, bank accounts, and any investment holdings that are in his name only."

Mom nodded. She seemed so small and defeated at that moment, but then she straightened her back. "He was *my* husband. I can take care of a bit of paperwork!"

After Mom signed the probate papers, Jack said, "Cathryn, you've made the trip here, and if you'd like to save the time and money of doing this again later, I could draw up a durable power of attorney document for you."

Mom nodded in appreciation, as saving money was a good thing, so we moved forward with the durable power of attorney (DPOA) conversation. Jack made it clear that someone with a DPOA could act on her behalf in financial and medical matters if she requested it. The durable aspect was important; without it, the POA would terminate should she become incapacitated, and her children would have to go to court to petition for authority over her affairs.

Without too much thought, Mom named me first on the list in her DPOA. Kate came second and Greg third. Greg, still on the phone, asked for clarification a couple of times but was quiet overall. I thought he was, as we were, oozing gratitude that this meeting was happening, that our lives might be a bit easier as a result.

We thanked Jack for the productive meeting, for his efficiency, and we left.

A few days later, I was walking out of a grocery store, and a call came from the 306 area code; that was Mom's area, so I took the call.

"Liz, it's Jack Neuman."

I used my shoulder to join my phone to my ear and started putting groceries into the car. "Hi, Jack."

"This is an unusual call and off the record."

I sat down in the driver's seat. "All right."

"Your brother's been calling me. I'm sure he loves your mom, but I have to tell you, I'm not sure he has her best interests in mind."

"What is he saying?"

"He's questioning the DPOA, which I've already sent to all of you, and he's suspicious of you and Kate. He's threatening to sue me, but I've been around long enough to know he's after your mom's money. I just think you and Kate need to be careful."

I should've been angry, but I wasn't. I felt vindicated. I'd known Greg my whole life, I'd had dozens upon dozens of examples of his dishonesty and greed, yet I still had questioned my own judgment.

· · • · ·

DURING OUR LAST DAYS with Mom on this visit, Kate and I spent time trying to clean and declutter her house. As we worked, Mom knocked on the refrigerator and said, "Hello? Why aren't you talking to me?"

Kate whipped her head around to look at me. I held my breath and listened to Mom, squashing my flight response.

"It bothers me when the refrigerator is quiet. It means something's not quite right."

"Why?" I asked, and my body stiffened.

"I prefer it when it's making noise. It's telling me everything is fine."

"Or," I said, "maybe we just haven't opened the door to let warm air in and cold air out in a while, so the motor doesn't need to turn on." Nervous energy had pushed me out of my seat, and I was standing now.

"No. The refrigerator is hooked up to a separate set of wires," she said. She looked straight at me without the contortions I was used to seeing when she was delusional. I relaxed a little, tried not to show a reaction, and attempted to remain present.

"These wires go to the control room." She glanced up. "Where he governs activity."

My nerves got the best of me, and I could no longer play along. I started for the garage, in escape mode. "I think I might try to get the lawn mower started. Your lawn needs mowing."

Kate looked at me. "I'm going to get out for a walk before it rains."

I went with her on the walk instead of mowing. We walked and walked faster toward the ocean until the refrigerator man became wild and unreasonable . . . laughable. We walked until the refrigerator man tension turned into a laundry list of all the absurdities we'd lived through our whole lives.

We reached the ocean, where seagulls crooned and squawked. Salty wind whipped through our hair. We were alone with the smell of the sea, crab and clam shells sucked of life, and ocean plants decomposing on the beach. Yet the ocean's force lapping the sand calmed my tension-filled body. The sounds and smells reminded me of walking this same beach with my daughters and Dad, my girls squatting and poking at what the ocean had spit up. As we hiked the empty beach, a lone seagull landed on a piece of driftwood the size of a refrigerator and pecked at it.

· • ● • ·

THE NEXT DAY, MOM wanted to talk to me about putting together a will. This was something new. It would be important for me to listen and help her if I could.

She started for the guest room to get her paperwork and rounded the corner, and the refrigerator went silent. "Wait. No, I don't think *they* want me to do this. Maybe tomorrow," she said, stopping in her tracks.

"Who are 'they,' and how do you know what 'they' want you to do?" I asked.

She pointed to her right eye. I waited for her to say more, but she didn't.

I squinted as if looking for something in her eye. Her small, black pupil, like the lens of a camera, helped with focus, and her hazel iris, the aperture, adjusted for light allowed into the retina, or film, which her brain interpreted. Mom suggested that something in there, in her eye camera, could possibly answer my question of who the mysterious entity in charge was.

· • ● • ·

BACK AT HOME IN Minnesota, I talked with Mom two to three times a week. Kate and I called or texted each other to share what each of us had learned. Mom drove to the grocery store. She was cleaning and cooking. Someone had stolen Dad's wallet. She was leery of how he'd died. She missed him and recounted the helpful things he did for her. Dad had gone from number one evildoer in life to a mistreated deity in death.

Life seemed calm enough for me to start working again. I'd been away from my clients for too long since Dad's stroke. With no imminent travel, no anticipated lawyers' appointments or funeral home visits, and no current schemes to persuade a distrustful mother, I could get back to caring for my family, my clients, myself.

While I worked to help create workplace harmony, to help organizations make sense of themselves, I felt lost in my own life, lost as to who my parents were and how I still felt tethered to their dysfunction. Inside me, pushed down deep enough to ignore, were my grief for Dad and the issue of Mom and her safety.

One day when the fog in my head was clearing and my footing growing stabler, my phone rang at the end of a client meeting. It was Mom. I gave my client an apologetic look and answered the call as I walked to my car.

In one breath, she said, "Hi, hon—I think I want to move to Saint Paul and buy a small house—of course, I'd rather live with you if that's a possibility, but I *will not* live in an assisted-living home." Despite emphasizing that she would not live in an assisted-living home, she sounded sweet, if despondent.

My body stiffened. I tried to answer, but no sound came out.

"Okay, you mull it over, and we can talk again," she said. She was quick, as if she sensed my unease and wanted the call to be over as fast as I did.

"All right. I'll mull it over. Good idea," I managed to say.

I drove from my client's office to my home in Saint Paul, panicky and nauseous.

25

TAXES

AFTER MONTHS OF US trying, and Mom resisting our efforts, to set up at-home care, cleaning help, errand help, or food prep assistance, we'd basically given up. Then she asked me for help completing her taxes, presumably because she'd given me her durable power of attorney "for when the time comes."

But "when the time comes" is a bit of a gray area if the person needing help doesn't want the power of attorney designee to assume the role. She hadn't asked me to use it; she had in fact rejected the idea of adding me to her bank accounts, and I was left feeling unsure of my role. What was best for her? What was legal? The attorneys I contacted weren't helpful. I could activate my DPOA in certain circumstances, but Mom, of course, could remove me from the role at any time, a role Kate and I knew would be critical at some point.

Like the old, rusty lawn chairs on her deck, nothing unfolded with ease when it came to Mom.

I gathered the emotional strength required anytime I spoke to her. "I'll help with your taxes if we use an accountant to complete them."

Her taxes, and the need to file them in a different state, created a situation complex enough for me to think getting an accountant's help would be important.

"No! I asked you because *I do not want* to use an accountant."

"I'll help with your taxes if we use an accountant," I repeated.

"Let me think about it," she said.

Five rough phone calls and two weeks later, she gave her okay—I could arrange things with an accountant. I worried she'd forget that she had agreed.

· · • · ·

FROM SEA-TAC AIRPORT, BETWEEN Seattle and Tacoma, Kate drove and I navigated the way to Mom's house in Ocean Shores. Mom had been living alone for seven months since Dad passed. We'd thought she wouldn't make it seven days.

"Here we are," Kate said as she pulled the rental car up in front of Mom's garage. I noticed her shoulders reaching for her ears.

"Let's rent a house on the ocean and come back tomorrow," I said. "She may not realize we're a day late."

Kate smiled, and I took a moment to relish the thought, knowing full well we wouldn't do it.

We walked toward the front door of Mom's small one-story, two-bedroom light-blue house. It resembled the other pastel-colored houses on the curvy road about a half mile from the ocean. We stopped to check out the yard. The grass wasn't as long as I'd thought it would be, but the twelve evergreen bushes Dad had planted on the perimeter of the lawn looked rough and bare. The branches and twigs halfway up the trunks were brown and leafless. The still-green bottoms of the bushes, without Dad's care, showed no promise.

We knocked on the door, and she opened it with a smile. She was skin and bones but stood upright with her shoulders back, hands on her walker. She appeared healthy overall—her skin color enhanced by a bit of rouge, her hair combed and smooth, her attire clean. It all suggested a well-kept person, though years of mental illness and resistance to medical care had added at least a decade to her seventy-four years.

I hugged her with a light touch, unnerved by the sharp edges to her clavicle and shoulder blades, concerned I'd throw her off-balance or break a bone.

We found the house in decent shape overall. Maybe she *could* live alone. Maybe without Dad, she had to do more for herself and that was good for her.

But though the house was clean and dusted, we couldn't ignore the piles of papers that occupied most surfaces. There were hundreds, possibly thousands of requests for donations, kept on hand for reasons that remained a mystery. The organizations that sent Mom requests for money appealed to her emotions, the causes ranging from her lifelong love of animals to random, newfound interests like saving the US Social Security system from the United Nations. Mixed in with these pleas were important items we'd need, like account statements, tax information, and bills. There were also several unopened envelopes that contained dividend checks ranging from $20 to $400, delinquent payment letters, and checks written but not sent.

Important papers and checks mixed with fear-based marketing junk—it was so symbolic of her mind, I couldn't rein in my agitation. The clutter, the chaos of paperwork, suffocated me, and my breath shortened. If I decluttered and organized, I thought, perhaps I could fix a part of her.

· · • · ·

ONE MORNING, I WALKED into the kitchen and living room area and saw Kate ducking and darting like a mouse in the night. Head down, she glanced up when she heard me. A look of mischief covered her face.

"I'm gathering some of Mom's junk mail that we can take with us into town to recycle or toss," she said. "It'll only make a dent in the work to be done, but I've got to do it!"

"I'm in!" I immediately started thinning out the piles, all the while peeking up the hallway to make sure Mom wasn't coming. Each day from then on, we'd wake up and do it again before our usual early-morning coffee runs, feeling guilt and accomplishment at once. We laughed at the thought of Mom's junk mail scattered across Ocean Shores, all near coffee shops, in recycling receptacles.

· · • · ·

MOM AND I WORKED together around the kitchen table. We focused on getting through one set of piles while Kate attempted to hack into Dad's computer to address his business affairs online. Mom took a seat on a chair fitted with two pillows to add cushion where there was none. She agreed to make progress and throw out some junk. I stood next to her shredder, a purchase made for her by Dad, who had been concerned about her hands, she told us, and her frequent use of scissors to shred her papers. I was ready to make use of it. She required me to use it with any item that might identify her.

"Let's just recycle it all!" I said with enthusiasm.

"If we recycled it, with my address still there, might it come back to me?"

Ah, so this is her concern. "No, Mom, it won't."

"Still, I think it'd be better if we shredded it all."

Desperate to get to the wood surface, I first chose trinkets and trash gifts from the pile: return address labels, personalized notepads, cheap pens, bags, stationery. Things she'd received in acknowledgment of the donations she had made and in anticipation of donations yet to come.

Mom handed me an envelope from a predatory organization targeting seniors and asked, for the seven hundred thousandth time, "How about this one?"

I patiently repeated what I'd already told her several times. "Just pick a couple of organizations you really care about and throw out the rest. You've been put on a list based on your giving, and that list was sold to other organizations. You're easy prey, Mom."

"Yes, I suppose you're right." And she grabbed her checkbook to write out another donation.

I walked away. It was the best thing to do, to give myself a time-out. I told her I would look for the checkbook she told us she'd lost. It was one of many checkbooks, but an important one, and we'd done our best to locate it. She'd already searched the house, gone to the bank, accused a few innocents of theft, and searched the house again.

In Dad's little room, I found Kate on the phone with her husband, focused on breaking into Dad's computer. She sat on the bed typing in whatever DOS language Brian told her to type, then repeating it back.

I plopped my wound-up body down next to her and focused on my breath. I smelled Dad. My chest tightened and ached like it did just before a good cry. We hadn't expected him to die so soon, and it was difficult to absorb that he no longer had a physical presence with us.

After he'd died and I had journaled my memories, his life choices had become clearer to me. The impossible situation Kate and I found ourselves in after his stroke, as we took moral responsibility for Mom, was the impossible situation he'd lived in for decades. Putting myself in his situation, having to consider her life, her well-being, and her choices, I thought about Dad's situation differently. I hadn't walked a mile in his shoes, but I knew from research that there wasn't a cure or panacea to her madness. We'd all wanted her to take medicine, but we couldn't force it.

Mom had chosen to stay with him after the tragedy that was our time in France. Perhaps he felt guilty for what could have been his part in the onset of her illness. It's believed that a deeply disturbing experience can wake schizophrenia in a brain where it's sleeping. Was our time in

France, his drinking and belligerent behavior, the original trauma that buckled Mom's brain? It's hard to believe he didn't harbor deep guilt regarding the possibility.

In their final decades, Dad made a life with Mom that kept her safe and relatively calm. His only other option, which I'm not sure he considered, was to leave. For Dad and for Mom, for better or for worse, it was till death did them part.

As I lay on his bed next to Kate, Dad occupied the room in the way his aroma lingered. His clothes hung in the closet ready for wear, and his blood pressure medication sat on the shelf next to his anticoagulant medication, both bottles half empty or half full. Half-empty. Tears welled up.

You weren't supposed to die first.

Through my tears, I noticed an old briefcase of Dad's tucked in the corner of his closet. I hadn't noticed it before, and Kate and I had taken opportunities to go through Dad's things as much as we could. One of us would look in files or drawers, and one would listen for Mom. She didn't trust us, and finding us snooping could make things worse.

"What's in that briefcase?" I asked Kate.

Kate looked over her shoulder. "I don't know! It's locked, and I haven't had time to figure out how to open it. None of the keys here work on it. But I'm so curious."

Just then, Mom pushed her walker, which had a large, deep basket attached, into the room to the foot of Dad's bed. She had filled the basket with a two-foot-high stack of messy papers she thought might be important tax information.

As I made my way through the pile, on my hands and knees categorizing the documents as best I could, I felt stunned at Mom's willingness to let me in. Grief was hard to identify in her, as her demons wore her down. But she'd been having trouble sleeping. She would bring up Dad and then sigh, sinking her chest to her spine. Her ideas about how Dad died had turned wonky. Perhaps it was her grief that finally allowed me into her financial world.

"Our appointment with the accountant tomorrow is for 11:00 a.m.," I reminded Mom.

"What? What appointment? I didn't know we had an appointment!"

"Yes," I said, "we decided to see an accountant—you agreed to it."

I was certain this was it—she wouldn't go. I expected her to flip out and begin weaving a twisted tale of the danger of accountants, or how an accountant once wore plaid, and you know what that means, right?

She stared at me with her eyes narrowed, thinking. Then, "Oh yes, it does make sense to use an accountant," she said.

Kate and I let out large sighs of relief.

The next day, we made our trip to the accountant with only one incident. Mom asked us, in the meeting, to count all the pages of documents we were giving the accountants, of which there were hundreds, to be sure she got them all back. They might have other sinister plans for her paperwork.

Later back at the house, Mom made her way toward me and shoved an envelope in my direction. "What about this one?"

"Mom, you know my answer: recycle these requests for donations. You get too many of them."

"I can't do that. I've looked at the return address." Her eyebrows narrowed, and her lips tightened against her teeth.

Baffled, I said, "What do you mean?"

"The microchip." She pointed to her eye. "They know everything about me." She shambled her way to the couch where I was sitting and dropped down next to me.

"I don't want you to think I'm cuckoo," she said as she twirled her finger in circles around her temple. "But an eye doctor put a microchip in my right eye. Through this—" She pointed to her right eye again, not taking her gaze off me. "They can see what I see. You're lucky you can read things and not have people know what you've read!"

It was the same story she'd told me thirty-four years earlier. I waited for more.

"I think the church is involved in this somehow, but I haven't figured it out," she continued. "Also, my friend Mary, who referred me to the eye doctor, she's in on it too."

"You told me about the eye doctor . . . and the microchip. When I was thirteen."

"Really? I did?" Her eyebrows arched and her chin dipped.

"Is that why you wore the eye patch?" I tried to appear casual.

"Did I? I don't remember that."

"Yes, you did, sometimes while jogging in the basement."

"Mmmm, if so, then yes, that was probably what it was for."

I didn't take my own eyes off her, but in my peripheral vision was Kate, who'd heard the whole thing. She pretended to look down at what she was reading, but her eyes were on us, as Mom commanded our full attention.

"So, you see, when I look at one of these envelopes and see who it's from, they know I've seen it, and I can't ignore the request. They might take revenge."

"What do you mean, 'revenge'? What might they do?" I asked, concealing my growing panic.

"Well," she demanded, her eyes bulging, wild, "why is my checkbook missing? Why do I get such pains in my shoulder? And now, I have to go to the potty, and I sit down but nothing comes out, and it's because *they* wanted me to do something else."

It was the most she'd shared about her delusions in a long time, and it immediately reminded me of a conversation I'd once had with a mental health professional named Glen. Glen ran a residential program for folks with serious and persistent mental illness. I had spoken with him as part of my research before volunteering for the organization's board of directors.

When Glen asked why I was interested in mental health, I told him about how I'd been raised by a mom with untreated schizophrenia and a dad with alcoholism. I explained Mom in detail, expecting him to sympathize with how it must suck to have a mother who isn't available and never has been.

When I finished, he said, "What an amazing woman!"

I almost accepted his compliment. *Okay, yes, I'm amazing!* I thought.

He continued, "To have the courage and the wherewithal to live with such a mental illness and yet still function as well as she has! That's extraordinary."

I was stunned; I can only hope I didn't show it. But with that interaction with a person who had given his life and career to helping people with illnesses like Mom's, the frame of my viewfinder changed. I'd had the camera focused on the wrong person and hadn't realized it. And years later, it was happening again.

As her daughter, I should've always felt Glen's compassion for Mom. Maybe because I'm her daughter, often I did not.

26

DAUGHTERS RESPONSIBLE

MOM FELL. HER SKELETAL, seventy-six-year-old body smashed head- and hand-first onto concrete. Alone and banged up, she rode, by ambulance, to the closest hospital. A striking clementine-size protrusion popped out above her right eye. Black and blue painted half her face. Blood crept up her forearm from her hand. The skin on her thumb and wrist swelled to a smooth, round surface, a dramatic contrast to the flaccid folds elsewhere over her bones.

At the hospital, she said, "Everything is fine. I'm fine. I don't want any high tech."

They asked her whom to call. She gave them our names but fake numbers. A clever social worker found Kate through an internet search.

From across the country, Kate pleaded to the social worker, "Keep her there as long as you can!" Since we legally couldn't make decisions for her, our only plan had been to wait for an emergency that sent her to the hospital, which could lead to assisted living. If they released her, our chance to influence her living situation would vanish.

The hospital released Mom before we booked our flights. The social worker said, "It's okay. She agreed to in-home care!" Mom knew what to say, what people needed to hear. She'd likely smiled and discussed climate change with him too.

The responsibility of caring for Mom, who refused care, from across the country alternately gnawed and ravaged us; like a vulture, it circled, never left us alone. As her daughters, it was our job to take care of her. Ask anyone. Ask her neighbors. Ask our friends. Ask Officer Chase.

Officer Chase in Ocean Shores contacted me whenever Mom called the police. Mom called the police because someone stole her necklace . . . twenty years ago. Mom called the police to arrest a young handyman who wanted to replace Dad in her life; when she refused him, he'd rotted out the wood railing of her front steps. I don't think she told them about her omniscient refrigerator or the persecuting microchip in her eye. She'd be careful with that information.

After one visit, Officer Chase said the house smelled of urine. He thought I'd want to know that.

After the fall, I asked Officer Chase what to do. Would calling Adult Protective Services do any good? He agreed that alerting APS might help, and he'd call them.

We had hope, another possible plan of action, but continued to work within a system that was working against us. Nobody could force our mom, a seventy-six-pound, incontinent woman with schizophrenia who dragged a foot, to accept in-home care or move to assisted living. Despite these facts, she was fierce, had grit, and trusted no one.

APS asked Mom if she was comfortable living on her own. She said yes.

That was all they needed to leave her and her situation alone.

· · • · ·

KATE ARRANGED TO SEND Mom's Meals, a relatively tasty and nutritious frozen meal program, to Mom weekly. Mom said she'd accept a cleaning person in her home after I told her APS required it (they didn't), and I'd pay for it.

I researched and arranged to phone interview a cleaning person in Ocean Shores named Evie.

"Hi, Evie, it's Liz," I began, thinking I'd start with small talk. But before I could get any further, she started fast talking in a rough, deep voice.

"I've been sober for twelve years," she said. "I clean rooms at a hotel, I'm honest, and I'm always on time."

I appreciated her direct approach and figured that not just anyone was going to make it working for Mom. I was ready to say, "Congratulations on your sobriety. When can you start work?" But I thought I'd better let her know what she was getting into.

"So, I need to let you know a bit about my mom. Physically, she has a hard time getting around. She uses a walker and I imagine needs help cleaning her floors, her toilet, changing her sheets, that sort of thing. She might also need help with errands, though she's still driving."

"Well, heck, I can do all that. I was working at a small hotel, and I cleaned all the rooms myself."

"You should know she can be difficult. She has a tough time trusting people."

"Oh, I know people like that. In my line of work and in my AA groups, there are plenty of difficult people, but I get along with everyone."

"Well, it might be more than that. You might expect that she'll accuse you of stealing. She might follow you around and give you instructions on how to clean and what products to use."

"Okay. Good to know."

"Also, I'll be paying you, but we don't want her to know too much about that because she might refuse based on how much you are paid."

"Roger that."

"Thanks, Evie. Your references were terrific, and I just hope Mom lets you into her house!"

We arranged for a day and time for Evie to show up. I called Mom to be sure she was still willing. She said she was. Then I waited, from a thousand miles away, to hear how it went, to hear that all the things I'd warned Evie would happen did.

Evie called after the arranged time and said Mom wouldn't let her in the house. Mom said she didn't need help, that she was perfectly capable of dusting, cleaning her floors, and doing her own laundry. "I hate to tell you this," she added, "but your mom smelled really bad, like old urine."

Friends and colleagues asked how Mom was doing. What to say? Not many wanted to hear the truth, but I couldn't say she was fine. My family knew I was struggling. My daughters made cards for me, for Mom, and often asked how she was. I went to sleep every night thinking about her, alone, shuffling around her house, talking to her refrigerator, peeing on herself, heating up frozen meals. I sent fresh fruit and cheese baskets. I sent adult diapers but had no idea if she used them, if they fit her tiny body, if the pee poured out the gap between the diaper and her leg.

Guilt and concern for her safety slowly consumed me. I worried about what would happen if her next emergency didn't land her in the hospital. After consulting each other's work and family calendars, Kate and I planned another trip to visit Mom. We tried never to go alone, without the support of the other. We were responsible daughters or daughters responsible. One of those. Did it matter which?

27

OIL AND WATER

ONE DAY IN EARLY March, I dropped my kids off at school and pulled over on a residential road to answer a call from a local number, not someone in my contacts.

"Hi, Liz. Scott Pearson here. Remember me?"

Scott, Greg's oldest childhood friend. "I remember you! Hi, Scott."

"Gosh, Liz . . ."

"What's up?"

He started to speak, and his voice caught. "I'll just say it. I'm sorry. Greg is dead. Gisela found him on their couch this morning." He wept.

The pain in his sobs brought my own tears. I was crying for Scott's pain.

Scott explained that he thought Greg might've died from an overdose. Greg would run out of his prescription narcotics weeks before he could get refills, and he'd fall apart, desperate for money, for drugs. He had a pattern of reaching out to Scott when things were bad, badgering him with aggressive language, phone calls, visits. Scott had always been there for Greg, and Greg abused that relationship. A few months before,

Greg had stopped calling during the rough patches, and Scott learned Greg was getting drugs from the street.

Greg, feeling terrible pain and in the throes of withdrawal, had indeed gotten street drugs just two days before his death. He paid a stranger who came to their door $300 for a bottle of pills. Two days later, he died on their couch while Gisela was running errands. The autopsy revealed he'd suffered an aortic dissection.

· · • · ·

TWO MONTHS BEFORE GREG died, I auditioned for a performance of storytellers called *Listen to Your Mother—Twin Cities*. Twelve stories of motherhood, funny and heartbreaking, told from a stage one night near Mother's Day, in a sold-out seven-hundred-person theater in Minneapolis. Cast to talk about my journey of awareness regarding Mom's schizophrenia, I would be delivering a public telling of a story we'd kept private for so long. I struggled with whether it was my story to tell. If Mom didn't acknowledge her illness, could I?

I feared that Greg, who lived nearby, would show up and cause a scene, playing the hero, protecting Mom. He had been antagonizing Kate and me through novella-length text and voice messages. I worried my involvement in *Listen to Your Mother* would give him the fight he wanted.

Now he was dead. He wouldn't be showing up for any reason.

I feared how Mom would react to Greg's death, less than three years after Dad's. I was a mother, and losing a child was my worst nightmare. I thought of Sandy-Mom and the unbearable blow of Mike's death followed by the forever ache of a hollowed heart.

I arranged to have someone Mom knew from a church in Ocean Shores be at her house when Kate and I phoned with the news. We didn't want her to be alone, I suppose the same way Sandy-Mom had not wanted me to be alone. She'd spoken with Greg, instead of calling me, and given him the news that Mike had died so I wouldn't have to be alone when I heard.

Once we knew Mom had company, we conference called her home.

"Mom, we have some terrible news," I said.

"What is it?"

Kate spoke. "Greg is dead. Gisela found him. He died on his couch."

"Oh no . . ." Her voice trailed off. "It can't be."

"I'm so sorry. I wish we could be there with you. It's such a shock," I said.

"It's terrible. Just terrible news," Mom said. She then told us she had company, and we'd talk later, but she never brought up Greg again.

At the funeral service in the Saint Paul area, Greg's ashes, in a blue urn that would've matched his eyes, were easy to miss despite their location at the front of the room. The minister stood to the right of the urn, and on the left stood a trifold with photos that Gisela, Teri, Kate, Greg's daughters, and my kids had put together for the occasion—fifty-one years of Greg. A giant, dazzling flower spray overshadowed a few small arrangements. The room otherwise appeared plain, like a convention center conference room, including a movable partition wall in the center.

Flanked by my family in the first row, I side-hugged my eight-year-old son and held my husband's hand. My two daughters, now ten and thirteen, sat on the other side of my son. Kate sat next to my daughters. Mom did not come. Ultimately, it was too difficult for her to travel.

As the funeral started, I felt no tears welling up, no inability to think straight, nothing that would prevent me from speaking at my brother's funeral. So then I thought I should speak, that I should say something profound about the loss of my brother, about his tough breaks, his bad choices. I turned and saw my three best friends, who had never met Greg, sitting on the other side of the aisle. While I was glad for their presence, I also wished they weren't there. Ambivalence complicated my grief, and I longed for a simple ending, with no witnesses.

What right did I have to speak? I continued to think about this as the minister droned on. In the past several years, Greg had become more unpredictable, angry, and accusatory. While we were connected by blood and childhood, as an adult, I had built self-preservation levees. I couldn't understand why he kept making bad choices. Decades of bad choices. A river in a flood of bad choices. He never learned from his mistakes. He never accepted responsibility for his actions. He never decided to choose differently the next time.

Had I decided to speak at the service, what would I have said? I could've conveyed more than what the minister said, which went something like, "Yes, he was human, and humans aren't perfect, so let's just talk about his love of electronics and cars." But with nothing prepared, I sat, mired in mixed emotions, waiting for it all to end.

Why are funerals and truth often like oil and water? People aren't comfortable speaking the truth about our dead—not so soon anyway. The minister relayed superficial bits of Greg's life he had learned only the day before. Shouldn't he have been exploring what made Greg tick, what he might've done with his gifts and why he hadn't? I didn't really expect a stranger to ask or answer these weighty questions, but they seemed to me appropriate for the heaviness of a funeral. If not at a funeral, when?

As I considered the stranger-minister's shortcomings, I realized I could've spoken about things that would make Greg three-dimensional. Like when we were young and our homelife was volatile. Our parents were each dealt a hand that, when combined, might've caused them to fold at some point and walk their separate ways. Their cards included intelligence and education, yes, but also poverty, war, refugee status, immigration, a serious brain illness, alcoholism, and a suicide attempt.

I could've spoken about how Greg and I used to love movies. Movies transported us, gave us the giddy, excited feelings of possibility, of how bad people could change and be good. One of those movies was *Mary Poppins*.

I thought about the time when after watching *Mary Poppins*, Greg and I gathered our change and got on our bikes, his with plastic streamers flapping, with our sights set on kite supplies. We were going to build ourselves some cool kites that would reach the atmosphere. On our bikes, riding down the Fremont Street sidewalk, we sang, "Let's Go Fly a Kite." Greg looked back at me smiling grandly as we screamed the words to the neighborhood. The screaming felt incredible; the expulsion of anger and fear in favor of the possibility of flight.

· · • · ·

AS I SAT THERE surrounded by all things death, Greg's death, my heart armored up and protected me from pain and yet allowed me to feel sadness for others, mostly for his wife and daughters. I glanced at an old friend of Greg's who was weeping so hard he couldn't catch his breath. Why was I dry-eyed?

I'd learned early in life to quell the hard stuff in favor of moving forward or beyond, but always away from what hurt. *Just get through today, go to sleep, and tomorrow might be better. No one needs my emotions; they never help.* This self-care had become instinctual.

I had cried it all out in France.

Instincts had kicked in the minute I received the call about Greg dying. A loss more complicated than the loss of my dad. Maybe I believed Greg didn't deserve my pain? That he'd hurt me so much already. Maybe I knew I'd blow up into pieces if I accessed all the emotions that seemed to be intertwined in our relationship. The anger / pain / injustice / fear / disappointment / secondhand shame had been locked and loaded for years, and this was not the time to pull the trigger. Not in front of my kids. Not when it might hurt too much for me to be the same afterward.

We'd had it rough with our parents; lots of kids do. I could have spoken at the service about how the roughness hit Greg harder than it did Kate and me. Perhaps he'd felt all those hard things, the ones I kept suppressed, and the avenues he used to feel better ultimately made him and those close to him feel much, much worse.

I'd grown up to believe each of us is responsible for our own development. That we all are free to grow. I grabbed onto this existentialist thinking as a philosophical theory to help me find a way out of my upbringing. We can create ourselves each day, the past is the past, and the possibilities are almost limitless. I applied this concept to my own life and personal growth after leaving home. The climb to self-actualization need not be a ruthless one; it might be a thoughtful series of steps taken to leave a cycle of dysfunction. We are in charge of ourselves and can decide on the direction of our lives. Was this too much to expect from my brother, who grew up with the same privileges as well as the same mental illness assaults as I had? Maybe so.

While I didn't feel the loss of Greg as one would expect, or like those who talked with him daily, I did feel a deep sadness for what could've been. I'd hoped for years he would change, like he and I had, after watching movies, hoped our parents would. But the possibilities that inspired us when we were young didn't play out for Greg in life.

I sat at the funeral listening to the minister's empty words. I looked around again and realized how few people had come to say goodbye. Some remembered Greg from our kite-making days. Most were there for his wife.

I considered the possibility that Greg was dealt a hand he couldn't find a way to win with, much like our parents had been. Like them, he had refused to acknowledge his illness, to make different choices, so no one had been able to help. I couldn't say I understood his methods in life, but how else can I explain them?

The minister finished with the Lord's Prayer. My relief that it was over changed to remorse. The opportunity to speak had passed, my private eulogy was left for the written page. I've decided to break my complicated levees and end with something genuine but simple: my hope is that he is now soaring like a kite in the atmosphere, pain-free, up where the air is clear.

28

HOVERING BUGS

A COUPLE OF MONTHS after the funeral, Kate and I entered Mom's unlocked house and held back gag reflexes as we worry-smiled at Mom, who didn't move from her padded chair in the kitchen.

She smiled. "Well, look! How nice of you to pop by!" Like we lived down the street or in the same state and not across the country.

We wanted to greet her, hug her, but large Mom's Meals boxes overflowing with moldy food blocked the hallway. It was a knee-high berm of Styrofoam: half-opened containers with bluish-green, hairy apple crisps, Salisbury steaks, and chicken pot pies, food that never made it to the freezer but that she had ravaged.

We maneuvered around the boxes. My shoes stuck to the faux wood floor, and with each step, I thought, *Where is that smell coming from?*

Mom wore a housecoat, front open to below her bare breasts. Tight skin covered each identifiable rib, reminding me of the mummy at the science museum, the one with the dark flesh tight against each bone, the one that kept my daughter up all night after she saw it. Mom's feet and ankles, also exposed and swollen red and purple, looked uncomfortable even though she denied feeling pain. More jarring was the realization that she'd lost awareness of something important to her: her modesty and appearance.

I thought, *This is it! She can't live this way. She can't think she can live this way!* And then, my heart took off and my words flew. "This is awful! Mom, it smells so bad here. Food is rotting everywhere. You can't live this way!"

She looked at me, eyebrows high, then looked at Kate. Kate pinched her nose and nodded. Mom looked back at me. She smiled softly. "I'm doing fine, and I don't smell anything. Your noses are too sensitive."

I tried a new approach. "Aunt Carol is in a really nice assisted-living home now, Mom. Would you consider living with Carol?"

"What? What did her daughters do?" Her eyes flared.

"No, Mom, it's not like that. Carol was wandering, getting lost in her own neighborhood, and could no longer take care of herself."

"That might be what her daughters told you. But I know. My sister does *not* need to be in a nursing home, nor do I!"

"It's assisted living. It's different," I said, though I wasn't sure why I even tried.

Kate opened the sliding glass door for air and mouthed to me, *I can't stay here much longer.*

Dragging her right foot as she had for years, Mom walked her skeletal body inch by inch toward her bedroom. I followed her and found a primary source of the stench: her mattresses. Soaked through. The floorboards near her bed were warped. Towels and small, sticky white pellets filled the washer and dryer. Forever frugal Mom was attempting to wash her disposable adult diapers.

While she wasn't looking, we threw out urine-soaked towels, moldy food, and garbage spilling out of small plastic bags. The hovering bugs, we hoped, would follow. We hurried out to purchase surgical masks and cleaning supplies from the local hardware store. We needed a new plan.

Mom agreed to let us clean, but she wouldn't let us throw anything out, including the soaked mattresses. Our new plan included Kate getting Mom out of the house for at least three hours. While she was gone, I'd clean and purge. It was an honest-to-god toss-up which was worse, but I was pretty sure I drew the shorter stick.

I called Evie, the cleaning person I had interviewed a couple of months earlier but who Mom had refused services from. She said she'd come help me and bring cleaning supplies. I'd supply the masks.

Shortly after, Kate called the doctor's office using her speakerphone. Officer Chase, our partner in getting Mom help, had suggested that if a doctor deemed Mom unable to live safely on her own, they could help us get her someplace safe. But on the phone, when Kate mentioned that we wanted the doctor to assess whether Mom should be living on her own, the clinic responded with, "We can't discuss that with you."

Kate said, "Okay, I understand privacy laws, but could you please just make a notation to the doctor that we're worried about our mom, and we'd like him to consider our concern as he assesses her?"

"I'm sorry, we can't do that."

This one-star-rated clinic was the only one in town. This one-star-rated doctor was the only doctor at the clinic. To take Mom somewhere else would require a forty-minute drive, and we worried about her pee leaking on the seats of the rental car if she had to travel that far. Either way, we didn't know anyone in the area. We couldn't use our network to help us get to a recommended doctor to help us get Mom someplace safe and sanitary.

Withered by disappointment but propelled by crisis, we decided to count on the doctor seeing for himself that Mom shouldn't live alone. Imagine a woman of seventy-six years and about seventy-six pounds who drags a foot and barely walks with a walker into your office. She smells of urine and has bursting red-and-purple sausages for feet. I held out hope he'd be sensible and have her transferred directly to a hospital or nursing home, or that at least we'd be able to get him to write a letter regarding his concern.

Mom agreed to go with Kate to the family doctor to have her feet examined, despite her leeriness. Kate offered to take her to a restaurant afterward and drive to the ocean to sit and eat.

After they left, Evie pulled into Mom's driveway in a beat-up old pickup truck. She stepped out and stood tall and strong. She wore ice-blue eyeliner and had dark, curly hair swept back in a red bandanna. Looking like Rosie the Riveter after thirty years of shipyard labor, she tried to keep her generous smile from moving over the top of her large, white dentures.

I rushed out to greet her and said, "Are you sure you're ready for this?"

In her rough, crackly voice, fine-tuned by years of cigarettes, she said, "Happy to help, ready to dive in." No small talk and no questions asked.

After over three hours of fast-paced mopping, washing, dumpster trips, moving the mattresses to the side of the house, and calling for a special garbage pickup, Evie and I got the text from Kate that she was bringing Mom home. I paid Evie and said goodbye, then waited outside. While the house smelled a bit better, I needed the fresh air.

· · • · ·

MOM AND KATE PULLED up shortly after Evie left. Kate stood next to me as we watched Mom make her way inside. She asked, "Wanna walk?"

Kate started off briskly, and I caught up so I could hear her better. "The pee smell was so bad on Mom at the doctor's office."

Kate, talking with her hands, now continued, "She looked so frazzled, unkempt like a homeless person, and she reeked. I thought it could only help our cause."

"Right." I was eager to see where this was going.

"The doctor, a bald guy about forty, asked Mom about her feet, like how long they'd been discolored and swollen and if they caused her pain. Mom explained her drop foot diagnosis and how she wasn't in pain but had a troublesome time getting around."

We rounded the corner toward the ocean and spotted some deer, who didn't bother to move when we approached.

"So then Mom smiled and complimented his shoes. He told her they were custom made for him. Mom said, 'Well, they just don't make things like they used to, do they?' The doctor looked at a file on his lap. And get this!" Kate was on fire now. "He told her she was in the low-normal range for her body mass index!" She threw her hands in the air.

 "Why on earth did he say she was in the low-normal range when she's clearly skin and bones?"

I looked down at the street and shook my head, having realized this doctor was not going to help us help Mom.

"Mom said, 'Yes, I do try to get as many calories as I can, but I expend so many just getting around the house with this walker.' Liz, she leaned toward him and tilted her head, eyes wide."

"Oh my god! Was she flirting?" I wasn't really surprised.

"Seemed like it. The doc recommended that she try Ensure to get more nutrients and calories in her diet, and Mom acted like that was a grand idea! Even though she's refused to drink the cases of Ensure we've already bought her."

"Ugh!" We were walking on sand now, and it was hard to move as fast as we wanted to.

"The doc changed the subject back to her feet. Without touching her once, he said, 'I'd like to give you a referral for a vascular surgeon.'"

I opened my mouth, but nothing came out.

"Mom didn't miss a beat before asking, 'And what will a vascular surgeon do?' He looked at her, her feet, and said, 'No, I don't suppose surgery would be a promising idea.' And that was it! He never commented on her status of living alone. He didn't mention any concerns, and he didn't try to talk with me alone. I think he is a small-town family doctor, and he didn't want to get involved."

29

MAY THE FOURTH

"I LEAK A LITTLE."

Maybe it was the magnitude of Mom's understatement, or maybe it was how she'd delivered the words with a sheepish grin, holding herself like a child. Whatever the reason, her words hovered over me as I tried to fall asleep back in Minnesota. I couldn't stop them, and I realized I couldn't ignore them.

As we waited for the worst-case scenario, Evie, whom Mom now let into the house three times a week to deliver groceries and help with cleaning and laundry, called to tell me Mom had lost the ability to walk. She couldn't get up from a seated position by herself and had agreed to go to the ER. My immediate and urgent phone call to the hospital requesting they admit Mom until we got there was ignored. She could no longer stand due to her sausage feet, a weak knee, and lack of muscle, yet there was no diagnosis by which to admit her to the hospital. Still, Kate and I purchased plane tickets, certain this time Mom would agree to move.

The Olympic Area Agency on Aging might've been the most helpful of the many organizations we contacted for help. We stopped with our prepared list of questions and challenges on our drive to Ocean Shores from the airport. The agency, tucked in a two-story building that housed an Anytime Fitness and a chiropractor and was next door to a Dollar Tree, was difficult to find.

The manager of the agency, Mark—a disheveled, earnest man with a yogi's calm—greeted Kate and me after we arrived. He had sensed our desperation from my phone call and now ushered us to his office.

We relayed our situation with our own earnestness, like we were the only ones ever to suffer so, and waited for him to wave a magic wand, give us the secret code, or summon an angel. What we got instead was a mantra.

He sat back in his chair. "There is nothing you can do. Or should I say, you've done everything you can do. I've been doing this work for years, since having to go through something similar with my mom. Though most people you encounter will disagree, you might find you just have to wait."

"Wait? For what?" I asked.

"The law is set up to protect the independence of individuals. Would *you* want to be forced out of your home to live away from most of your things, be told what to do and when, and have strangers bathe you?"

"Right. No, we understand. It's just . . . it's hard to wait, not knowing what kind of emergency will occur, and people don't understand that we can't do anything," Kate said.

"We even contacted Adult Protection Services, and they didn't do anything," I added.

"I can tell you stories, stories of situations much worse than your mom's," Mark said. "The mom of the CEO of a large Seattle corporation wouldn't answer the door for APS. She spoke to them out her window wearing just a T-shirt, nothing else. She was completely incontinent. But she told them she was fine, so they left. There is just not much they can do."

The idea of suing for guardianship, to make Mom's decisions for her, came up again. Mark confirmed what we'd already learned: it would be an ugly, lengthy process, the result certainly not a sure thing, and frankly, we didn't have that kind of time, nor did he think it would work.

"Help isn't help if it's not wanted," Mark said. "Safety and cleanliness are no longer her priorities, though they may be yours."

True. Yet nagging at us and complicating the matter was her schizophrenic thinking. Who was telling her living in a safer, cleaner environment wasn't a priority?

We left Mark's office without answers, but he had waved a magic wand of sorts. We were under a brief spell of relief, knowing we'd done all we could. He'd seen cases much worse than ours, and all we could do was wait. Again, wait for the worst-case scenario. "It is what it is," he said. This became our mantra. Our secret code.

Kate and I gauged the success of our days with Mom by items added to and checked off our lists. Evie didn't have time to clean much, so we scrubbed and purged. The cleaning Mom appreciated; the purging we did while she slept. We arranged for her house to be made safer and wheelchair-friendly by having grab bars and poles installed and removing high thresholds. We thought she might want to stop using the unstable floor lamp to steady her descent into bed or her rise to the wheelchair. She resisted these changes even as they were happening and subsequently refused to use the room after the installation of the suspicious transfer pole.

We arranged to have Evie come three times a day. Mom, now somewhat comfortable with Evie, agreed with this plan.

After a week, we left Mom, wheelchair-bound and in Evie's care, and flew home. Evie texted us daily, sharing her hours, receipts from grocery purchases, details of what Mom ate, and other happenings, like that Mom had taught her some French, let Evie wash her hair, or was being "testy."

"Testy" began to appear in at least every other text to describe Mom after just a couple of weeks. Their honeymoon was over. Mom needed her more than three times a day. Evie reluctantly obliged. Then Mom started calling Evie, who lived twenty minutes away, as if she were pushing a nurse or flight attendant button. Evie grumbled. I worried she couldn't get sick or take a day off, and if she did, we had no backup plan. If there was a fire, Mom couldn't get out of the house, as she couldn't transfer herself from couch to wheelchair.

On each of her visits, to assist Mom with toileting, scrappy Evie, untrained in personal care, placed a bucket and a large pad by the couch, helped Mom stand, and held her by her armpits while Mom released her urine and poo . . . all on top of the beloved Oriental rug that Chou Chou, our white fluff ball of a dog, had also relieved himself on.

Evie kept Mom's bum clean and attended to a sore on her butt, with wound care supplies sent by Kate. For a while, Evie was happy Mom could no longer get to the washing machine to wash the disposable diapers, which caused a terrible mess. Then Mom began to find her way around better with the wheelchair and had access once more to the laundry area.

We paid our angel Evie well, and she needed the money. But this wasn't sustainable. By early March, Kate and Evie both agreed with me: they would support my renewed efforts to get Mom to assisted living.

The thought of talking to assisted-living homes about Mom without sharing everything about her paralyzed Kate. If they knew about her schizophrenia, they might try to put her on medications before letting her in, which would endlessly complicate our task. In fact, it would make it impossible. And then there was the challenge of actually working with Mom to get her to move.

Through most of my life, I'd been content to sit back and let others lead. I'd also been fighting my inertia and fears for years. By opening the blinds, illuminating the elephant in the room, I had helped bring about positive change at work and at home. I'd addressed conflict and had difficult conversations when no one else would. It was time to put those new skills to work for Mom, whether she wanted it or not. I would get her to a safe and clean living situation. I wouldn't engage my escape parachute, and I wouldn't stop until Mom was in a well-run assisted-living facility. Waiting for disaster had left me haggard. The former fuzziness of what to do—what was right or wrong, legal or illegal, moral or immoral—became clear to me, and I had a goal. I dropped "It is what it is" and picked up Kate's baton of action.

I researched facilities in Washington and learned the process for admission. When Kate and I learned Mom could no longer walk, our first call was to an assisted-living home just a couple of miles from Mom's house. As Kate had feared, they told us Mom would have to undergo a psychiatric evaluation and be put on medications before she could be admitted. We didn't want to add this to our already long list of impossible tasks, so we kept looking.

After researching several alternatives between Ocean Shores and Seattle, I settled on the assisted living with memory care in Seattle where Aunt Carol lived. My cousins were happy with it, and Aunt Carol living there might help Mom accept the idea.

I spoke with Beth, the sales representative for the assisted-living home, while I was on spring break at an Arizona dude ranch with my family. I sat squinting in the bright sun, ordered an IPA, and gazed at Saguaro National Park. My goal was to explain Mom's behaviors without scaring her away with a label like *schizophrenia*. Mom wasn't dangerous, and her illness now came across as mild dementia doused with paranoia. Maybe her schizophrenia didn't need to be addressed. Indeed, it hadn't been for twenty-eight years.

"Mom can be difficult," I started. "I'm not even sure how we would get her to you. She has a very strong will. She values her independence and her dignity, of course. She's incontinent and can't walk anymore but doesn't need any skilled nursing care and doesn't take any medications."

"This sounds very much like many of our residents here," said Beth. Her cheerful, smooth voice sounded positive and empathetic. I took a gulp of my IPA and swallowed the bitterness with relief.

"Oh, that's good. Our cousins told us a lot about your facility, but I still wasn't sure she'd be right for your home."

"What else can you tell me about your mom?" She was upbeat and sounded genuinely interested.

"Well, she typically has a soft demeanor. She likes to argue about current events, speaks French, and she loves animals. But she can also be distrustful. She accuses people of stealing her things." The sun had moved, and the hundreds of saguaros cast dark shadows.

"Well, I think it would be wonderful to have the sisters, Cathy and Carol, in the same facility!" said Beth. "And we've seen it all. I'm sure our staff would be great with your mom."

"What will I need to do next? What is the process?" This is the part I dreaded.

"I'll send you intake forms. We'll also need a form filled out by her doctor, and she'll have to have a TB test. After that, an apartment will be waiting for her!"

I spent hours filling out the intake forms, finding the fine line between truth and omission, delivering relevant, helpful information that wouldn't also disqualify her. The final requirements for admission were a completed form from her doctor and a TB test. One of our biggest hurdles had always been getting Mom, fearful of high tech and medicine, to the doctor. How could I do this from Minnesota in short order? The one-star doctor who saw her the previous July had moved out of Ocean Shores. We saw this as a positive, but it also left us with no personal doctor on record.

After sharing this new obstacle in a conference call with Evie and Kate, Evie said, "I can get her to the new doctor in town."

I was surprised and thrilled. But doubt prompted me to develop a relationship with the clinic manager. "Please, this is so important. She can't know we're arranging to have her go to assisted living, and she absolutely needs a TB test. Can you help me?"

The clinic supervisor shared with me the eldercare struggles she had with her mom a thousand miles away. She understood, and she'd take care of things.

Between Evie and me, we made several doctor's appointments for Mom. Each time Mom, or the refrigerator, decided she should cancel. After the fourth appointment in three weeks, she went.

Evie contacted me as they were leaving Mom's house, and I notified the clinic manager.

After, Evie relayed to us that it had been a rough visit at the clinic, and despite both our efforts, they had let Mom leave without the required TB test. Luckily, Evie managed to get Mom back a couple of weeks later to render a negative for TB. The doctor noted on the form for the memory care facility that Mom had signs of dementia. There was no mention of a psych evaluation or medication she'd refuse to take. We had everything we needed.

Everything except Mom's willingness to go.

· · • · ·

KATE AND I BOUGHT one-way tickets, left our families and our work, and flew back to Seattle in early May.

We made our first stop a tour of the assisted-living home, which was in a beautiful neighborhood in Seattle. It was quaint, cottage-like, a place we thought Mom might like. We sat with Aunt Carol during a sing-along. She smiled at us, though she didn't know who we were, as she held the verses to "America the Beautiful" and pretended to read them, singing from the part of her memory still intact.

On our drive to Ocean Shores, Kate and I ran through ideas about how to persuade Mom to move. We settled on a plan that required Evie to help us deceive Mom. We were nervous—Evie had gotten close to Mom. Would she lie for us? She was on board with the plan so far, but it could make things exceedingly difficult if she had a problem, like I had, with the deception.

Mom was vulnerable and legally independent. Yet everyone agreed that what we were doing was overdue and in her best interest. Since my confusing childhood, I'd found straightforwardness and clarity the most comfortable path, even in the face of conflict. We'd tried to be direct, and it didn't work. Ultimately, my need to have her someplace safe overwhelmed my aversion to lying.

Evie, however, was giving up a good-paying job in a town with a depressed economy. I could not discount that this fact might make the next steps harder for her. She'd have to deceive Mom to lose her job.

We arranged to meet her at our favorite restaurant in Ocean Shores, a place where the bartender knew us, where we had crab salads and margaritas every time we visited. We hugged Evie and sat down. I launched in.

"This is how we see things going with Mom. Please let us know what you think. Tomorrow or the next day, we'll sit down with Mom and tell her you need to visit your sister."

Evie smiled, her top lip slipping above her shiny false teeth. "I do need to visit my sister and nephew in Michigan."

"Great. Since we don't have a backup for you, we will tell her we've arranged to take her to stay with Carol in Seattle while you're away. Mom must realize she can't eat, move, or clean herself without your help."

Evie, still with her coat on, nodded. "Well. I don't think this is going to work."

My heart raced. "Why not?"

"You all can't do it in her house. You need to get her in your car before you tell her. She ain't gonna go otherwise."

Kate put her hand over her mouth. "Oh my gosh, you're right!"

For a bit, no one said anything. Kate's chin quivered. She started crying, and Evie reached her long arm around Kate's shaking shoulder.

Evie said, "You all are doing the right thing. It's hard, but it's right. I've been with your mom, and I know it's the right thing for her."

We decided we'd spend the next day with Mom, and the following morning, May 4, we'd take her on errands before driving her to Seattle, to her new home.

Evie, standing to leave, said, "I'll pack a few bags for her, things she'll want and need for a few days, and put them in the garage. While you're inside with your mom tomorrow, I'll put them in the back of your car."

After she left, I called my contact at the assisted-living home and said we hoped to have Mom there two days later. I arranged for Mom to get a furnished room for the first month, to give us time to decide what she'd need and collect it from her house after she was settled.

I called Mom's attorney, Jack, the one who'd drawn up her DPOA after Dad died and had raised concerns about Greg. I told him we'd be traveling near his office in a day or so, with any luck, and I wondered whether I could use my DPOA to make me or Kate the representative for Dad's estate instead of Mom. Sure, he said, he could arrange that. Why not? It might be our last chance. A drive-through lawyer's visit. Let's try to get all the remaining impossible things done in one day.

· · • · ·

WE SITUATED TWO LARGE absorbent pads under an old blanket for Mom in the front passenger's seat of the rental car. As promised, Evie put two packed suitcases in the trunk while we chatted with Mom in the house about our planned errands, including to her bank in Aberdeen to try once more to deposit Dad's checks into her account (another ruse to get us to the lawyer's office). She seemed eager to join us. Kate drove. I rode in the back seat, and we headed out of town on a mild, sunny day, no whirling wind, no cold gusts, just the bone chill of deception.

Kate's husband texted his support: "May the Fourth be with you!" His play on words made me think that, in addition to the Force, we could also use a lightsaber and a stormtrooper, please.

When we reached the bank, a Chase branch, Kate parked and I got out, said I'd be back in a few.

Once I was back in the car again, I sighed. "Well, darn it! They won't do it. They won't deposit Dad's checks into your account, Mom. Like Anchor Bank, their policy is that the checks have to be put in your name."

Mom frowned, her eyes darting back and forth. Before she could answer, I plunged ahead.

"If we make a stop at your lawyer's office two blocks away, you can sign some paperwork to begin to make that happen."

Her face brightened. "Why don't we do that?"

"I'll call to let them know we're coming." I grabbed my phone and immediately started typing the number before she could change her mind.

Mom said, "Maybe they could send someone down to the car with whatever I need to sign." Then, indignant at the thought they might refuse, she added, "Of course they could do that!"

Jack sent a notary down with the documents for Mom to sign. Mom, as expected, began to read them. "What is this?" she said. "No! I'm his wife! This is my responsibility."

"We'll be sure to give you the receipt of deposit afterward," Kate offered.

"Oh. That's sounds good. Yes. That's not too much to ask either now, is it?" She took the pen from the notary and signed the paperwork.

Kate continued driving. Mount Rainier, topped with white snow against the blue sky, came into view. Mom and I kept our eyes fixed on it, its permanence and immensity. Like the moon, it moved with us, and we noted how it never failed to take our breath away. Mom didn't mention, if she realized, that Mount Rainier isn't visible between Aberdeen and

Ocean Shores. She didn't ask where we were going, even as we passed by Olympia, where Dad had received treatment after his stroke.

The plan was that at some point during the 130-mile trip, I would tell Mom where we were taking her and why. I knew my job was drawing near, but I was enjoying the time with Mom, listening to her comment on the various sights we passed.

It had been about a year and a half since she'd traveled these roads with us. That time we took her to visit Carol in Seattle, before our cousins moved their mom to the assisted-living home. We'd met our cousins Gina and Carla and Aunt Carol for dinner. We'd all thought Mom, seeing Carol so far into her disease, would understand why Carol had never called or come to see her after Dad died.

Kate had hugged Carol, then warned me not to. Carol hadn't been bathing for months, and her foul scent lingered on Kate's clothes. In the restaurant, Carol sat across from Mom at a separate table, next to ours.

Carol stared at her hamburger. She had forgotten how to eat one. She asked for advice on the topic from Carla, who told her yes, it was a hamburger, and she could pick it up and eat it. Carol wasn't sure who we were, and instead of conversing, she recited poetry throughout dinner.

Afterward, Mom employed her Rice Sister Power of Denial and said, "Carol is just fine. Nothing wrong with her. I don't know what her daughters are talking about." We suggested Mom invite Carol to move in with her instead of to assisted living. Mom replied, "Oh. Sure." And then a moment later, "Well, I'm not so sure about that."

· · • · ·

WE WERE ABOUT AN hour away from our destination when Kate stared at me in the rearview mirror and mouthed, *Now*.

I sucked in some air and said, "Mom, we need to tell you something." Mom, still looking out the window, mumbled, "What?"

I was holding my breath. I had no choice; I had to follow through. "Evie needs to get away, to go visit her sister in Michigan for a few weeks."

Mom flung her head toward me and yelled, "What? That is terrible! How could Evie do that to me?"

I flinched. Mom hadn't yelled in a long time.

"Mom, Evie has not had a day off in over three months. She deserves to take time off. And I have good news! You can stay where Carol is staying until Evie comes back or until we have another plan."

"I'll think about it."

Kate, eyes on the road, waited a moment, then said, "I'm driving you to where Carol is staying now, Mom."

Mom stared out her window and said nothing. I said nothing. Kate said nothing.

Then, after more than thirty minutes of silence, we passed the headquarters for Boeing. Mom looked at the building and said, "I had my first office job at Boeing!" And with that, she commented on the sights again: the skyline changes, the traffic, the landscaping.

About thirty minutes after passing Boeing, Kate pulled the car up to the entrance to the assisted-living home. Mom looked out her window. "Where are we? What is this place?"

I stepped out of the back seat, retrieved Mom's wheelchair from the trunk, and positioned it by her door. Kate came around, and we transferred Mom to the chair. Mom stiffened her arms and scowled.

She looked at Kate and asked, "Where did you pick me up from this morning?"

"Your home in Ocean Shores."

"Well," she said, eyebrows high, "why aren't you taking me back there?"

We proceeded to tell her the story about Evie going out of town again and how we had arranged for her to have her own little apartment here, where Carol lives, until we figured something out.

"I have plenty of food at my house to last a few weeks!" she declared as if this were enough reason for us to scrap our plan.

I motioned for the representatives and caregivers, including an old dog, to come out and greet us. "But you can't get to your food, Mom."

"Oh, right, there is that." She smiled as she reached out and petted the golden retriever, who wagged his tail.

The caregivers took Mom to see her small apartment. She scowled. Then they offered to take her to see Carol. Yes! Mom would very much like to do that. We followed, as did the reminiscence coordinator, the activities coordinator, the lead nurse, and the admissions representative. No one wanted to miss this reunion.

The activities coordinator retrieved Carol from a room where a guitarist was playing. They told her, "Your sister, Cathy, is here."

Carol came to the wheelchair and grabbed Mom's arm. "It is so nice to see you! You look great. You are my longtime friend and colleague!"

Mom beamed. "You look well too, though I think we could both use a haircut." Mom laughed.

Carol's small smile stayed the same.

Mom asked, "What is your full name?"

Carol raised her chin high. "Carol Jane Rice!"

Mom's face brightened again. It seemed Carol had passed a test.

The admissions person had told me Carol had a cat in her apartment, so I asked, "Do you have a cat in your apartment, Aunt Carol?"

"This isn't a cat!" Mom exclaimed. "This is my sister!" She looked at me like I was nuts.

Everyone standing behind the reunion—the employees, Kate, and I—all had wet eyes. The staff escorted Mom and Carol to Carol's room, where they could have some time alone together.

Kate and I unpacked Mom's things and made a mental note of what we'd need to bring back for her on our way to the airport in a few days. Then we went with the director so I could sign her life away. Kate, the director, and I sat in a conference room along the hallway near the apartments. He had a stack of papers four inches high. The director spouted legal speak, but I wasn't tracking; it had taken all I had to get to this point, and I had nothing left. I started signing anyway, though the content of what I was signing went in one ear and out the other. I was waiting to feel relief from all we had accomplished, but I still felt jacked up. How could I be certain this would work? What if I'd been wrong in assuming she'd be no more of a hassle than any other resident with dementia? What if Mom had a psychotic episode and they decided they couldn't deal with her? I was continuing to sign, wishing I had an abbreviated signature, when a staff member wheeled Mom past the large glass wall separating the signing room from the hallway.

Mom looked in and saw me with pen in hand and a stack of paperwork on the table. She narrowed her eyes, opened her mouth, said something I couldn't hear, twisted her head back as her thin arm reached behind her chair toward the conference room door, toward us. The staff member continued to move her along.

· · • · ·

WE LEFT EXHAUSTED AND drove in a rainstorm through Seattle, back toward Ocean Shores, to clean out the house. Two blond, middle-aged, Norwegian Russian (or Russian Norwegian) zombies, having no idea, no training, no support, no clairvoyance that would tell them if what they'd spent themselves accomplishing was just.

"Was this the right thing?" Kate asked. "Is this going to work?"

Rain pounded the windshield, and the wipers missed a large area, blurring my view of the road. Over the city, electricity from the storm lit the dark sky around the Space Needle, where Mom and Dad, madly in love, had once spent a photo-worthy date. In the photo, and now, they are both dots in the distance.

"I guess only time will tell."

30

PURGING

BACK AT MOM AND Dad's house, after days of nonstop cleaning and sorting, Kate and I sat side by side, slumped on the stinky couch, staring blankly.

I fell to the side as Kate jumped up, scurried to Dad's office, and returned with the tattered and locked leather briefcase we'd both wondered about. "I've always wanted to know what was in here," she said as she gripped its frayed corner, managing to get her fingers inside to force it open. She reached in and pulled out a two-inch stack of double-sided typed pages.

A journal, written later in his life.

The potential for the answers that would anchor me tugged my chest, and I sat up straight. Would we learn why he drank, why he didn't get Mom help, and why he attempted suicide? Would I learn about how he viewed me? Who was I if I never learned these things? I leaned into Kate so we could read together.

Dad describes a scene in 1999, eighteen years earlier. He is sixty and leaving to spend a three-month sabbatical in Russia. This was when I took my trip to see Mom, when she told me about Dad fraying the bindings on the books, and when I started to change my mind and think about having children. In the journal, he and Mom drive in silence across brick roads through our small midwestern town to the Amtrak station. They bump along in the little Toyota with the baggage for Dad's three-month trip, their voices suffocated from resentment.

He boards the train at the station and peers out the window. She stands by their car with one hand on her hip, the other one waving. He evaluates the wave. Is it a hearty wave? Is she happy he's leaving? Or is it a sad, almost regretful wave that suggests she meant to say something kind before he walked away? Why wouldn't she wave the way she did when they were young and in love? Was she thinking of someone else?

He spells it out early: on this trip, he hopes to find himself, to better understand his identity, Russian or American. He also wants to decide if he should leave Mom. He does not mention her schizophrenia. How could he separate her from her diagnosis? And yet, that's what we all did. We'd anticipate a rational person and collapse when we got the illness instead.

The sobriety he had achieved just a few years before the sabbatical must've given life to the questions he'd drowned in alcohol during my childhood. As I read further in his journal, my heart sank with validation as he referred to that time as his "blackout years."

Kate and I read all the paragraphs Dad had marked out with black ink, by holding the paper up to the light. Then wished we hadn't. First sex romp with Mom in our grandparents' basement. Important memories for him, maybe, but ones we didn't need to read. He wrote nothing of suicide, of drinking, of resisting help for Mom. He wrote nothing about his children.

The journal didn't answer our questions, but it told me he was a regular guy who had survived a horrid childhood and who had missed out on a normal path to emotional maturity. He did the best he could with the faculties he had. I decided then that I would try harder to stop blaming him for ignoring my development and for not getting Mom help. He was not the person I'd put on the pedestal, and it was okay to lower him to the shaky ground with the rest of us.

While purging the house, I considered Mom's dust-covered trinkets and teacups, an eclectic mix of furniture, a urine-stained couch, and the well-traveled Oriental rug.

"Everything here has bad chi," I said. We needed to deal with her things, all of which, to me, held negative energy. From broken plates and expired food to the rug and teacups, all the items were invaluable to Mom. Her possessions, unlike her mind, were tangible, hard to deny or dispute. Her possessions held meaning, and it upset her to think about losing them. I think the items gave her memories weight in a brain where thoughts mostly floated untethered. They helped her in her arguments with herself, or maybe with Dad.

My eyes fell on Dad's tan lounge chair. Its cushion, formed to his backside, made it look like he had just gotten up to use the bathroom. Other things stopped time, like Dad's side table, which held remote controls to devices Mom never used, toenail clippers and four-year-old clipped nails, a French-English dictionary with pages yellowed at the edges, AAA batteries, and tissues, new and used.

"What do you think? Are we done here?" Kate handed me a bag of garbage to take outside.

As I walked with her toward the front door, bag in hand, my foot stuck briefly to the floor with each step. Trinkets, teacups, and bad chi still littered the place. Without our parents' memories, we had hoped to find something to explain their choices: our childhoods. That's what held value to us, but that's not what we found.

"Yes. I'm ready."

31

UNTETHERED

KATE AND I VISITED Mom regularly for the first three years she resided in assisted living, before the pandemic began in 2020. The first time I was allowed to visit Mom after COVID-19 restrictions lifted, it'd been over two years since I'd seen her, and I didn't know what I'd find. I tapped on her door just after 10:00 a.m. My middle child, Elena, who had traveled with me, stayed in the hallway while I peeked in and glanced toward the bed. The shades were drawn, and through the shadows, it was hard to make out Mom's tiny, barely eighty-pound figure, curled up under the blankets. A fall mat had been positioned on the floor where she'd dropped out a few times, to make sure she wouldn't break into pieces the next time. The rumpled covers might have masked the presence of her body had I not seen her white hair and gray face. She looked dead. My heart landed with a thud in my gut, and I shuffled backward out of the room.

My knees refused me full support as I joined Elena in the hallway. The caregivers I'd spoken to hadn't mentioned she'd declined. What to do? Wake her up? I didn't want to frighten or confuse her. I also didn't want Elena to witness Mom in distress.

Already, I was worried Mom wouldn't know who I was. I thought back to when, though I knew she had disjointed thinking and hallucinations, I had wanted her to be proud of me. I had wanted her to be compassionate toward me, to be loving, to make me feel safe. To behave in ways she was never able to. I don't believe I ever gave up longing for my mother's love. I had wanted her to like my friends, comfort me when Mike died, and be happy with my graduate school choice. To simply know me. She had given birth to me and otherwise took care of me for many years. She saw me take my first steps, play with other kids, learn to read, fear trains and school bullies who pulled my pants down. If I should be known by anyone, shouldn't it be by my mom? I had wanted my dad to know me and for me to know him too, and I had lamented that loss after he'd had his stroke. Why was this parent-child understanding of each other not possible in our family?

Elena and I walked down the green-and-gold-carpeted hall toward the dining area. The shared spaces smelled stale and rancid. I wondered if this was the smell of overcooked food mixed with incontinence, but I've read it's the chemical transformations humans go through during the aging process that change our odor. The collective nature of that smell can be overwhelming. It must have smelled this way on my other visits. Maybe I'd forgotten since so much time had passed, or maybe I was smelling it as if through Elena's nose.

Five residents sat in the English country home–styled living room, looking lost, staring into the air. One woman dressed in dark slacks, a pink sweater, and pearls strode up to me and in an energetic and familiar tone said, "I'm heading to town for groceries. I'll be back soon." A short, athletic-looking seventy-five-year-old woman in a tracksuit marched the hallways repeatedly, smiling, telling us each time she passed, "I think my family is here now. I just have to find them."

Whether it was a chemical change in the people or the kitchen smells, something made my stomach lurch as I told an employee clearing a table that we wanted to visit Mom.

She put some dirty dishes on a cart and studied me.

"My mom is still sleeping. Is this normal for her?"

The woman wiped her hand on her apron. "Cathy? We don't see her till close to lunchtime. She sleeps in."

A personal caregiver overheard and told me she'd have Mom up and ready for the day in an hour. Elena and I wanted to distance ourselves from the folks more vulnerable to germs and get some mask-free fresh air, so we waited outside in the car.

I had warned Elena before the trip that Grandma Cathy wouldn't likely recognize her, it had been so long since they'd seen each other. She also knew of Grandma's schizophrenic thinking. But in our phone calls with Mom, my kids thought she was funny. She laughed a lot and always ended the call saying, "Toodle-oo!" To them, she was entertaining, harmless Grandma.

I had worried about Elena seeing her grandma and the other residents, many of them unable to walk or speak. It can be hard on a kid to see elderly people in that state. But Elena was handling it well. She knew herself. All my kids seemed to know themselves and harbor a quiet confidence I've never known. I think Elena was worried about me, though I'd done my best to not show my angst.

I glanced at her in the passenger seat of the car, checking messages or TikTok on her phone. We'd visit a college later that day, and she'd chosen to wear a navy sweatshirt, purchased the night before, her cream painters-style pants, and black high-top Chuck Taylors. I wished I had been more focused on comfort when I was her age; as a teen, I didn't leave the house without spending an hour on hair and makeup.

At thirteen, I'd declared that I wouldn't have kids, afraid I'd become like Mom. Afraid I'd become disconnected with reality and not be a good parent. Afraid I'd pass along the mistakes, the inherited trauma of my parents. As it turns out, my children have made me a better, stronger version of myself. I haven't done everything right; my upbringing has found its way into my parenting, as I'd feared, but only in small ways. It's not about getting it all right, I've told myself. It's about loving our kids, providing a safe and nurturing environment for them to grow up in, and knowing them better than anyone else does. Someone once wrote to me that there is no way that we, as parents, can fix all the mistakes of the past in just one generation, no matter how hard we try. I'm happy to report that we can make a hell of lot of progress.

After an hour waiting in the car, Elena and I walked back to Mom's room and arrived as her caregiver was wheeling Mom into the hallway. Her white hair was clean and shiny. It fell into a bob around her small, still-striking face. A pink shirt underneath her dark wool sweater brightened her complexion. I sighed with relief. She looked 100 percent better than she had in bed. Don't we all?

I wheeled her into the small conference room along the hallway, between her room and the dining room: the one with the windows facing the hall, the one where I'd spent hours in zombie mode signing the paperwork on the day, over four years prior, we moved her in.

"Who are you?" she asked after we positioned ourselves around the corner of the table. Her eyes were inquisitive and kind.

I lowered my mask so she could see my most distinguishing features—my nose and my smile. I waited a moment. Her expression didn't change. "I'm Liz. Liza. Lizabeth. Your daughter. Kate couldn't make it this time." I'd had to come without her, something I had vowed to never do. "This is my middle child, Elena."

Mom nodded. "You both look like you could be a relative of some sort."

I almost laughed, my chest tightened, and I started to gasp under my mask. There was no air to suck in, so I took off my mask in panic. She smiled at me, unaware. Her bony hands made fists, and she held her thumbs tightly between her index and middle finger. It looked uncomfortable, as if she might not be able to relax them.

Across the table, Elena didn't flinch. But she did raise her eyebrows at me.

After catching some air, I put my mask back on and turned to Mom. "How do you like living here?"

"Oh, it's nice. I like it very much."

"You sleep well?" I wondered about her tendency to sleep late in the morning.

She whispered, "No," and looked to the side, toward the door.

"Why is that? Do you get enough to eat?"

"I don't know why I can't sleep. But I eat whenever I want to!" She laughed.

Elena's sweatshirt had PIKE'S PLACE printed on it, and Mom asked about it. We told her we'd been there the night before. We talked about the Great Wheel on the waterfront and how Elena and I had ridden it as we had eight years before. We told Mom how we'd laughed as we changed spots on the wheel mid-ride to re-create a photo I took when she was eight. Mom spoke fondly of the Seattle area and Puget Sound. But when I asked her about her family of origin, her only sibling, Carol, she didn't remember them either. My cousins had moved Carol, who had gotten much worse off, to another facility, but Mom had not interacted with Carol in years. Mom told us she had a big family, several brothers and sisters. Not a minute later, Mom's eyes darkened. "Who are you?"

"I'm Liz. I'm your daughter."

"You look like you could be related to one of my daughters."

"Oh! Which one?"

"Oh, it doesn't matter." She moved her gaze toward the door again.

"Well, I am one of your daughters. I'm Liz." I moved my mask down again and left it there. We were speaking as strangers, and while it often seemed that way with Mom, this time was different. Dementia was not reversable, and schizophrenia can be treated. There was now no hope for finding what we'd never had.

"You could be one of Liz's daughters."

I smiled. Without the baggage of being her daughter, I realized our interaction had lost the weight and angst that had permeated a lifetime of conversations. All the unsaid between us, her inability to trust me, all we'd failed to know about each other, all the ways she had failed to be a mother—and I, a daughter—didn't seem to matter. The painful longings and resentments were wiped clean the instant she didn't recognize me, and the result was a deep, brutal release.

She looked at Elena's shirt. "You have a Pike's Place shirt on. Have you been?"

"Yeah, we were there last night," Elena said in her soft, calm voice.

I told her my older daughter, another one of her granddaughters, Katya, was in college now, and her Russian professor knew Dad and had collaborated with him on a few projects. The professor had known him as Bill Fiedorow, not Vasily Fyoderov, and had told Katya that her grandfather was a legend at Knox College.

Mom smiled in a new way, with her whole face, with tenderness and full recognition. Recollection sparked in her now warm eyes. "Oh! Lots of people called him Bill. He also had, or has, a great memory and was good with languages." She didn't know if Dad was still alive or not, but she remembered him. Fondly, not with the anger and pain that had defined their marriage. Not with the memory of how they had made each other miserable but would never separate for good. I had wanted them to divorce when I was young. Yet they had stayed together till death parted them. I didn't understand either of them, nor did I understand their enduring love. My version of a camera's zoom mechanism, my attempt to make sense of my parents through writing, hadn't offered the clarity I'd hoped for. They will forever be dots in the distance.

The exploration, the investigation, had, however, helped me understand that I had built a life, one in which I'd developed some courage and self-acceptance, even without the foundation of understanding their choices. Maybe it was, in fact, because of their choices and the challenges their parenting had left me that I had been able to find my voice and my ability to create something different in my own family.

I looked at my watch and realized we were late for a college tour. I looked at Mom. "I think it's about time for us to go. Or should we stay longer?"

"Oh, I think we've had enough. Don't you?" Her shoulders dropped, and she relaxed her tight fist.

We wheeled her to the living room, where *The Golden Girls* was playing on TV. I reached down to give her a hug, and she patted my arm awkwardly as if I were someone she'd just met.

"Goodbye, then," she said.

Elena and I walked out, into the rain, and stood together by the car. She gave me a look of love mixed with concern and then put her arms around me and squeezed hard. It was a fierce hug. The kind of hug that takes your breath away and then recalibrates it to that of the hugger. I clung for a moment, soaking up my daughter's maternal warmth and the soft water droplets before climbing once again into the driver's seat.

Mom and Dad at a West Seattle High School dance around 1957.

Mom and Dad heading off for their honeymoon in 1960.

Kate, Liz(a), and Greg in France 1974.

ACKNOWLEDGMENTS

MY OLDER SISTER, KATE, and I are six years apart, our childhoods linked, but not the same. I thank her for taking me in when it mattered for my life's trajectory, her celebration of my writing, her affirmation of my memories, and for sharing her own details with me for this book.

In 2016, I auditioned to tell a private story in public. Thank you to Galit Breen and Vikki Reich for casting me in the 2016 *Listen to Your Mother* Twin Cities performance. I experienced how telling our stories, even stigmatized ones, heals and connects us.

To a Minneapolis treasure, The Loft Literary Center, and the beautiful connections I made in classes, cohorting with Nicole Helget's 2018 Memoir Project writers, and basking in the glow of the 2021 Mentor Series Fellowship and trying to absorb bits of brilliance from mentors Anika Fajardo and Kiese Laymon. To my fellow CNFers, Irna Landrum, Maureen Ramirez, and Kou Thao.

Out of The Loft Literary center experiences came writing groups. Thank you, Kim Sabow, Catherine Squires, Anne Winkler-Morey, and so many more.

Any writer's dream team, Jenifer Fennell, Holly Gross, Ann Hohenshell, and Rhonda Ray, carried me gently yet expertly across the finish line. Extra thanks to Jen for her part in saving me from the ghost of unpublished manuscripts.

· · • · ·

THIS BOOK WAS TOUCHED by generous and gifted writing teachers, authors, and mentors including Anitra Budd, Laura Flynn, Nicole Helget, and Kate St. Vincent Vogl. I owe a deep gratitude to early readers including Debra deNoyelles, Kate Gjerde, Barb Larkin, and Susan Ritt. With key comments and encouragement, they ushered me to the next level.

Thanks to good friends Jodi Benson and Sarah Hayes Jewell for their encouragement and generosity while listening to and reading early versions of my work. And to Kate Tilney and Maureen Wosepka for their enduring support for me and this project.

To my friends who invigorated me with the lift of laughter and conversation, pickleball and tennis trash talk, therapy walk-and-talks, cabin weekends, bike rides, book clubbing, boot camp sessions, trail clearing, and hikes in the woods. The joy we experienced together while I wrote and edited this book was essential to my well-being.

To all the beautiful and generous people who allowed me to give their characters their real names. It's a vulnerable place to be, in a memoir, particularly one you didn't write, and I thank you for that sacrifice.

Memoir isn't meant to include everything and everyone in someone's life. My story skips over amazing experiences with so many important people I could never list them all. I hope you know who you are.

To Wise Ink Media for choosing to publish *You're Too Young to Understand* and for all their expertise along the way. In particular thank you to my guiding light, Hanna Kjeldbjerg. Every office hours session with Hanna is a joyful master class in publishing.

Finally, thanks most of all to my husband, John, and our kids Katya Marlena, Elena Rane, and Elliot Odin. We've created a family built on compassion, togetherness, and hugs. I love the way we tease, challenge, and support each other. Thanks for allowing me to tell stories with you in them.

In memory of Mike Cross, Vasily Fiedorow, and Marlene Sjaastad. I hope they hang out together sometimes.

DISCUSSION / REFLECTION QUESTIONS

THE BOOK OPENS WITH an end-of-life issue that Liz and her family face. What makes this situation complicated?

EARLY IN THE BOOK, Liz(a) and her family live in France. Liz surmises later that her dad's drinking and verbal abuse might have triggered her mom's schizophrenia. How did you think about their separate illnesses and their impact on one another?

WHEN DID YOU REALIZE Liz's mom had a mental illness? Did you suspect schizophrenia? What were the signs and symptoms? What did you know about schizophrenia before reading this book?

LIZ SUGGESTS THAT, LATER in life, she'd learn about what happened when their family left their dad in France. What did you think might have happened when they left?

AFTER COLLEGE, WHEN LIZ learns what happened to her dad after they left him in France, she wrote that it clarified some things about her childhood. What do you think those things could be?

WAS THERE ANYTHING ABOUT Liz's young teenage shenanigans that surprised you? Why?

WHAT IMPACT DO YOU think Liz's dad's experience as a child in WWII had on his life, marriage, and being a father?

DOES UNDERSTANDING WHAT HAPPENED to Liz's father in childhood help you feel compassion for his behavior in adulthood? Why or why not?

HOW DO YOU THINK Liz's dad's Russian heritage impacted his life and the lives of his family members?

PARENTING HAS CHANGED A lot since the 1970s and 1980s. How does this knowledge impact your view of what Liz and her siblings experienced?

WHAT WAS YOUR REACTION to the chapter where Liz tells her brother's girlfriend that he's cheating on her? Was it the right thing to do? It starts with a big decision and ends very differently than expected. What was your reaction?

LIZ ENTERS A RELATIONSHIP with John after a tragic event. It provides her comfort and sleep, but this budding relationship was also deeply confusing for them both. What were you thinking as you read this section?

IF YOU WERE LIZ or Kate, would you have tried to get your mother to resume treatment after she came home from the hospital and stopped taking her medications? What might you have done differently?

DO YOU THINK THE stigma surrounding mental illness and alcoholism is as prevalent now as it was when these events took place? How have social and medical views changed?

HOW DID HER MOTHER'S schizophrenia impact Liz and the rest of the family while they lived together?

HOW DID HER FATHER'S alcoholism impact Liz and the rest of the family when they lived together?

LIZ TRIES TO UNDERSTAND her brother and his choices in life. Do you believe they were choices? Was a different path available to him?

DISCUSS HOW GROWING UP with adversity, like Liz did, can impact one's values and behaviors in adulthood.

SHOULD LAWS BE MODIFIED to allow us to force more people with serious and persistent mental illness to receive treatment for their illness? How did Liz's story affect your views on this?

KATE AND LIZ STRUGGLED with being responsible for their mom but being legally unable to help her. Is there an ethical way to change this?

HOW COULD LAWS OR practices be modified to help families decide on when to end life-sustaining treatments for their loved ones?

IF YOU COULD ASK any character a question, what would it be?

HOW DO THE CHARACTERS' pasts influence their actions and decisions in the story?

IF YOU COULD GIVE a piece of advice to any character, what would it be?

WHICH CHARACTER'S ACTIONS OR decisions did you find the most surprising or unexpected?

WHAT WAS YOUR FAVORITE scene or moment in the book? Why did it stand out to you?

ABOUT THE AUTHOR

LIZABETH FIEDOROW SJAASTAD WAS born in 1967 and grew up in Galesburg, Illinois. She received her BA from Knox College in 1989 and her MS from Loyola University Chicago in 1992. After a career in organization development, Liz began writing. She received Minneapolis's Loft Literary Center's Mentor Series Fellowship in 2021. She has published in *The Sun* magazine, *Motherwell Magazine*, and WritersDigest.com. This is her first book.

    Her life story has inspired more than just a book—it has fueled her advocacy. Liz spent seven years on the board of Touchstone Mental Health, is currently active with NAMI, and continues to share her voice to build awareness of schizophrenia to help end the stigma that prevents understanding, research, and important changes for those suffering. To keep up with her journey or find resources, visit her online at **lizsjaastad.com and Instagram: @lizsjaastad**.

Liz Sjaastad, her mom, Cathryn, and her daughter, Elena, during a visit to Cathryn's assisted living facility.